TRANSFORMATION

THE LIGHT OF KRISHNAMURTI

Walking Together in Truth

DR. HUBERT WALTER KELLER

Published by Divine Light Publishing
P.O. Box 1110, Gleneden Beach, Oregon 97388
jayasarada@aol.com

ISBN: 978-1893037-33-5

Library of Congress Control Number: 2023901396

Cover design and interior layout:
Deborah Perdue: www.illuminationgraphics.com
in collaboration with Arielle Beauduy

Editors: Joni Wilson, Patricia Frances, and Arielle Beauduy

Cover photo by D. Wadia, Krishnamurti in 1948.
Courtesy of Krishnamurti Foundation of America (KFA) ©KFA

The Beginning

If you have been guided to read this book, then most likely you are searching for a truth, reality, or an understanding of life deeper than your daily experience. Paradoxically, the first step in discovering this truth is to realize what is *not* true. If you stop for a moment and just sit in silence, you can observe what is *not* true in your life.

Are you, in fact, the separate transient story that you have been writing since your birth? Are you your patterns of reactivity and fear? Are you your projections upon yourself and others? This book advances the position that these thoughts and emotions don't represent your deepest self.

We are rarely guided toward or able to look at our life's essence, which is not subject to time and outer conditions. Most of us have created and identified with a sense of self that is based in our past conditioning, memories and beliefs, and the projected images of others. Layered upon this foundation of "self" is our history of successes and failures in trying to obtain something or become someone. This pattern of seeking a sense of self in the outer world is really the root of all sorrow. This first chapter will discuss this root of sorrow and its relevance to what is actually true in our life, but normally hidden by our false identity. So, being ignorant means we start by examining our everyday assumptions and maybe laying them aside.

In our observation of life, we see that on the surface it is a manifestation of duality. That is, existence seems to always appear in pairs of opposites such as birth and death, pain and pleasure, night and day, and so on. The everyday mind also thinks in terms of duality. That is, achievement and loss, happiness and sadness, good and bad, joy and sorrow, love and hate. We are constantly swayed by the pulls of these psychological opposites and unfortunately, this becomes the mechanism by which we live. For most of us, life is spent chasing desires for the positive pole of these opposites, which are really just thoughts we have about reality. And we find ourselves running from the painful or negative aspect of these pairs. Usually our desire for the one leads us into contact with the other, which our desire, thought or judgment, has actually created.

This way of being causes a constant relationship with the past as we analyze our actions to determine if we have attained the desired result. And we project ourselves into the future as we plan to attain what has eluded us thus far. This common outlook rarely allows us to just be in the simple moment-to-moment experience of life.

In our split consciousness, half comprised of what we know of ourselves in the past, and the other half what we are projecting ourselves to be or become in the future, we create an identity that is totally based on thought. We even create an additional layer by inflicting judgment upon this thought-based split consciousness. Our identity becomes a split sense of self fueled and driven by judgment, as we judge whether or not we are succeeding or making mistakes in obtaining our desires. When we experience the pleasurable side of duality, our self-worth is enhanced. When we feel what we call the unpleasant side of duality, we often have low self-esteem. These are both caused by deriving an identity from the outer world, and from our psychological conditioning, also from outside. When we believe our low sense of self is our true nature, we believe in these thoughts and emotions that feed that negative sense of self. When we believe in the thoughts and emotions, they likewise feed our low self-esteem and the process forms a kind of cycle or circle.

Consciousness when allowed to be free of opposites, and of negative and positive judgments, is still, empty and can be realized as the source of our true being. There is an urgent quest that is now guiding us to return to our original and natural state of consciousness prior to thought or beyond thought. We are guided to unravel the layers of false identity and meet the source of life itself. We are compelled to let go of our false self, as we believe it to be on the surface, turning our attention inward and asking the most profound question in life, "Who am I?" This question when asked seriously opens the mind to true self-inquiry and gently allows the unraveling of false identification to take place. In deep self-inquiry, it is possible to simply ask this question and let the answer appear. One can simply ask, "Who am I" without my past, my history, my role in life, my gender and so forth. That is, all the thoughts you might have about your past and future. Invite your mind to be silent, receptive and willing to see and experience your true life in this moment and begin standing in your own pure life energy. The source of your true nature is found in the eternal essence of who you are beyond worldly conditioning.

—Jaya Sarada

Contents

CHAPTER 1

Listening Anew

So, to listen differently, a new form of consciousness, a deeper, innate consciousness must be present. In rare moments, through actual experiences, man has experienced this deep, innate consciousness. At these times the real consciousness spontaneously fills the need. These are the conscious moments of resurrection, moments of rebirth.
This real consciousness is of another dimension—it is beyond fear, devoid of reaction. It is directness, action, the real.

In order that there may be a correct approach to the material in this book, it is important to bear in mind that there is the difficulty of understanding each other. Most of us listen to what we hear casually, and hear only what we want to hear (and let us, for simplicity, include reading when we refer to listening). We disregard that which is penetrating and disturbing, and listen only to the things which are pleasurable, satisfying. Surely there can be no real understanding of anything if we listen only to those things which gratify or soothe us. It is quite an art to listen to what we hear or read without prejudgment, without building up defenses against those things with which we disagree. We should try to set aside our acquired knowledge, our idiosyncrasies, and points of view, and find out the truth of what we hear.

Most of us believe we know how to listen and take it for granted that we only need to concentrate, to be free of distractions, in order to understand what we hear. Nothing is further from fact. Actually, we do not know how to listen, and our present manner of listening is false. It prevents us from understanding the true significance of that which is being presented.

The problem does not exist in the simple act of being attentive. This is not the vital factor, for it is but the "tuning in" of the physio-psychic mechanism. Physical attention is basic and necessary, but mental-emotional attention is not basic, for it is both false and obstructive to understanding. Physical attention should of course be free of distractions, both inner and outer environment, but what is most significant and absolutely essential is the form of consciousness with which we listen. The mind with which we listen, and the manner and means with which it meets and uses that which is being heard, is of primary importance. The vital factor is the attitude of mind with which we listen, what consciousness consists of when we listen, and what consciousness does with what it hears.

The act of hearing consists of the physiological reception and transmission of neural impressions of vibrations of the air, which are conducted by the auditory mechanism to the brain. There they are received, registered and interpreted as sound-neural designations with no psychological qualifications. This last is done by the psychological part of the intellect.

Thus, the act of listening is both the act of hearing and a functional process in and of consciousness in which the response to what is heard will be in keeping with the functional capacity and nature of that consciousness. Our present functional process of listening is one of consciousness in constant reaction; that is, it is psychological response, a protective reaction. As such we use all physical, emotional and mental experiences on an intellectual comparative basis. What we consider best for ourselves, we consider to be "fact." So all impressions, whether originating from outside or the inside, instantly undergo interpretation and modification by our acquired psychological self-protective consciousness. Our present consciousness consists of a conditioned value of comfort and security, resulting from experiences of pleasure and pain. Our psychological mind changes and uses all functions to aid and support its concepts and conclusions, hence distorting natural function and creating illusions out of itself. Psychological mind superimposes upon the normal functions distortions founded upon falsely conceived concepts of certainty and security. Not only listening but all our functions, the physical, the emotional, the mental, have become instruments of psychological protection.

Thus, our process of listening consists of the protective activity of the intellectual, interpretative form of consciousness. All sound impressions, and in this case ideas and information, are grasped and interpreted in terms of itself, its combined concepts and feeling reactions. So, we listen as a psychological self-protective consciousness, in which our thought is, for us, the criterion of reality. As such, all ideas and other stimuli from the outside are met by ideas from the inside, and the outside is converted to comply with the inside, or the inside is made to conform to the outside. As such, all responses are only adjustments, modifications and conversions based on self-satisfaction or self-protection. They are ideas and feeling reactions resulting from the psychological mind serving its own aims and ends.

When you listen to another, you listen through the screen of your own conclusions, of your own experiences, of your own knowledge. You listen to confirm your beliefs and to strengthen your opinions. You may listen in order to obtain a new method of thinking, a new psychology; or you may listen to refute, to find fault and error in what you hear. You may listen with condescending curiosity, rather than with serious intent. Or you may listen in order to improve and exalt yourself in relationship with others. Regardless of what causes you to listen, if it is born of acquisitive motivation, it stems from protective desire. You do not listen to something new with the new, but with the old; hence it is extremely difficult to understand what you hear fully and completely.

There is a correct way of listening, especially to something that may be foreign; something that may be new, that you may be hearing for the first time. But when you listen to something new, you are apt to brush it aside as not understandable, or you are apt to be too quick in your judgment. Whereas if you can listen anew, you will comprehend much more than by merely listening through the screen of your own prejudices and impressions.

So, if we want to understand each other, we must listen very attentively not only to the verbal expression, but also to what the words are wanting to convey. Words are inherently limited, and ideas are only an arrangement of these limitations. So, communication and the possibility of communion is more important than words and ideas, more important than the act of verbalization. There can be communication between people only if there is real intent to understand.

If you do not want to understand, if you merely criticize, verbalize, intellectualize, there can be no communication or communion. But there will be communication, deep, wise, extensive, if there is the real intent to understand. Real intent to understand is far more important than the facility to philosophize; to psychologize, to criticize, to discuss or learn a new way of expressing a thought. But before there can be real intent to understand, there must be the realization of the necessity to put aside your conclusions and opinions. You must realize that your present approach and use of psychological self-protective ideas are false and valueless. Then you may be able to approach what you read here with a neutral attitude of mind, one that is quiet, free of ready criticism and conclusions. Then there is the possibility of listening with an attitude of freshness, with a mind unburdened, intensely absorbed, as when listening to music. Then you will be able to allow communication to unfold, following it through without expecting to gain anything.

In the beginning this will seem impossible, because your immediate and usual response to anything new is to question the validity of anything that controls your opinions and concepts. Your protective process of living consists of learning, getting, having, "being something," and defending this "something" at all costs.

We move from achievement and accumulative motivation. We fulfill through acquisition, possession and retention. This is the process of your present consciousness; hence it will be extremely difficult for you to approach the present subject matter openly, free of contention. Because of the tenacious character of the intellectual process, you will most likely greet, without knowing it, all that you hear or read either by interpreting it in keeping with your previously established concepts and using the new to confirm and expand them; or you will do the opposite. You will accept the new totally, and then set out to abandon what you formerly held to be true. If you do this, you will only strengthen your present way of thinking and feeling.

Your difficulty is that you will want to deny and destroy the old, or you will want to translate the new into the old so that you can make use of it in your relationships, making it practical, "worthwhile." What is important is not to put the new into the old. Let it remain new, whatever it is. Let that very newness operate, and it will. It will destroy the old because the new is so very vital, clear, abundant. If you let it operate, as it will, according to its own way, you will find it is highly practical. It brings its own action. Therefore, bring nothing to it. Do not add it to that which you know. Do not use it to destroy the old. Allow it to be unchanged, unmodified. It will reveal itself. You must be very alert not to intrude your present thinking processes upon that which is being presented. To do this you must be free of psychological thought, self-protective thought, even if it is but for the moment. This will be possible when you know how to listen.

So, to listen differently, a new form of consciousness, a deeper, innate consciousness must be present. In rare moments, through actual experiences, man has experienced this deep, innate consciousness. In critical and desperate situations, which he has been totally helpless to solve or free himself, suddenly and seemingly from nowhere, the solution has presented itself. When there has been a great shock, a crisis and severe suffering; when the intellect has had a desperately critical problem it was unable to solve; when a man's intellectual mind was completely baffled, and he knew it, then the intellect became quiet and relinquished its control and resistance. Then protection ceased. At these times the real consciousness spontaneously fills the need. These are the conscious moments of resurrection, moments of rebirth. This real consciousness is of another dimension—it is beyond fear, devoid of reaction. It is directness, action, the real.

We have called these experiences "miracles" and often attribute them to divine intervention. They were nothing of the sort. They were simply real consciousness in action. It is an experience possible to anyone, for it has occurred in the scientific laboratory, on the battlefront, in the desert, on the deathbed. These experiences have shown us the way we could meet life. But we have not recognized the significance and real worth of these experiences, for they have not changed our way of thinking and feeling, our way of living. We continue to live as a security-seeking consciousness. As this protective consciousness is always first to meet and instantly officiate at all experiences, it constantly obstructs and prevents the manifestation of real consciousness. So it is evident that if you are to have that which is real in you, it will be necessary for you to free yourself from your false psychological process of thinking.

Listening anew is not a new method or process of listening. It consists of being free of the present method of listening, free of the intellectual comparative process of thinking, free of memory; consciousness wiped clean like a slate. You will listen anew only when you are free of your present process of listening. This study is entirely concerned with the barriers that at present obstruct our ability to listen anew and therefore to live anew.

To live anew it will first be necessary for you to wake up, to become conscious of the barriers to understanding. For this to take place, you must first familiarize yourself with these barriers, then actually experience them in yourself and see their cause.

This requires a fundamental change in consciousness—a change from all self-protectiveness to openness and real inquiry. The purpose of this study is for you to experience your falsities, to awaken you, to produce shock and crisis. If possible, it should produce spontaneous interest and intent, an openness and inquiry and a deep realization of need. There must be the experience of psychological consciousness being these falsities and also their cause. It will require conscious elements that are not of the psychological process to expose it, for without them, the intellect will not allow denudement. Denudement of intellect is necessary to experience that this psychological consciousness is the cause of these falsities.

In the beginning it will be most difficult to be open, for man is a closed process, a protective process. His intent and inquiry will contain, unknown to him, some form of achievement motivation. But if you are serious, you can try to be open, and by recognizing these achievement motivations you can become aware of how closed you are. You can then give undivided attention and listen with as little resistance as possible. If you can listen without trying to gain something from what you hear and read; if you can listen without comparing it to what you know; if you can listen without wanting it to be in keeping with what you know; if you can listen without wanting to do something with it; if you can listen without accepting or rejecting it; if you can just listen and leave it alone, then the significance of the new will appear, not at first as conscious understanding, but as conscious awakening. And when you awaken to what is false in you, there is the possibility of experiencing it in yourself, of being these falsities in consciousness, discerning and understanding them, and thus being freed from them. If you can maintain an attitude of continual listening anew, if you can follow it through, it will break the hold of the old and bring it to an end without your conscious effort.

The new is taking place all the time if you are listening. But the greatest difficulty is to listen and to die every moment to that which we are, the old. We must be awakened to see the old in ourselves, and in this awakening, die to the old. In so doing, you will see a rebirth taking place. There will be no vacuity, no emptiness, no loss, but rather an extraordinary sense of creative being which, if allowed to operate, will solve all problems, however complex, intricate and pressing they may be.

CHAPTER 2

Two Ways of Looking

Consciousness is the process of living and dying from moment to moment. We must understand and be the birth and death of experience as consciousness.

There are two ways of looking at life. The ordinary way is to see life as manifest in the universe, in religion and science, in politics, in the emotional or mechanical. There is another way of looking at life, not as manifested in the universe but as a process taking place in the individual. Please see this point clearly. The process that is at work in the universe or in the individual cannot be understood except as it is seen in you, the individual. If you are truly to understand that which is about you, you must first understand that which is you.

In all physical manifestations we see the outer evidence of constant change in which everything is coming into being or is returning to its primary state. Nothing is static, everything is in constant change. It is either in a process of being born, being formed, growing, fulfilling, or it is dying, disintegrating, going through decay and returning to primary substance. All is completing a cycle of manifestation, appearing, disappearing, being and not being. In this we see there is a definite period of manifestation for all things. For the Essen, one-millionth of a second; for a white blood cell about twenty-four hours; for a dog a few years, and so on. For man a few years of physical life, but for thought, consciousness, and the experience of it, only the instant, the moment it is taking place. The period of consciousness, and the possibility of experience is only in the moment of pristine manifestation, and never afterward. Hence the possibility of experience of actuality, reality in man, and the understanding of it, can take place only in the very moment of its original presence in consciousness. You cannot intellectualize your experience, think about it and then understand it.

Fundamental change is the living quality of life. This change denies that there can be a static personal center, the "I," which is accumulating, storing up memories as safeguards and virtues;

a center which is constantly gathering experience to itself, gathering the lessons for the future. We must see the necessity for the functioning of man's consciousness and the fulfillment of his living processes to be in keeping with this fundamental process of change. You must live constantly in the moment, in which there is constant being and dying of experience, in which there is no carryover, no memory to guide, direct, dictate and demand. By so, doing you will then be able to experience the process of being and dying, the experience of fundamental change as the living quality of life.

Though intellectually we may grasp this, emotionally each one of us clings to a personal center, the "I," identifying himself with it. Conflict must inevitably arise when there is a static center within one while about one there are changing values. In reality there is no center, no "I" with permanent qualities. We must fully understand this, not merely intellectually, if we are to fundamentally alter our relationship with our neighbor.

Consciousness is the process of living and dying from moment to moment. We must understand and be the birth and death of experience as consciousness.

By being fully aware in the present, in the full consciousness of the moment, you experience all the entanglements, the psychological desires of the past and present. You will be aware of dormant hopes and longings, which surge forward and prevent you from functioning intelligently in the present. If you are aware of this, aware of it at its depth, not superficially, then the lack of understanding and incompleteness disappears. You will then meet each movement of environment, each challenge, each swiftness of thought, anew.

The establishment of an aim and intent is of primary importance for one who desires to disentangle himself from the complications of life—not the aim and intent of another, but an aim and intent that is born of one's own experiences, one's own sorrow, suffering and understanding. Such an aim and intent, when once established, will throw light on the confusion of all thought, and make clear the purpose of life.

Desire to see what really is, is needed for liberation from this confusion of thought in us and about us. The moralists are afraid of desire, thinking that it is something evil, which must be destroyed. But this is a mistaken attitude. Desire is the motive power behind all action. Desire is not the problem—the problem is the kind of desire, what desire is concerned with. There is manmade psychological desire, which is selfish desire, which results in all conflict and suffering in relationship. And there is real desire, which is the driving force of enlightenment and the eradication of selfish desire. It is the direction, use and action of desire that is significant, not desire itself. So, if you would fulfill life, you must have great desire, for desire brings experience, and experience leads to real knowledge. If a man knows how to use desire, it will bring him freedom. If real desire is killed, suppressed or perverted, there is no possibility of freedom. Most people in the world have intense burning, vital desire, but instead of using it correctly they, through conditioning, either suppress and pervert it or are controlled by it. Because man does not want or know how to be free, he kills his desire.

Right aim and intent is real desire, and this aim and intent must be created by you yourself. You must discover your own way of attainment. There is no other truth, no other god, but the aim and intent, which you have established for yourself.

You must also keep in mind that your aim and intent will be a variable. Your aim and intent can never be other than that of which you are conscious. Hence you cannot set for yourself an aim and intent suggested by another. You cannot set a goal of "pure being," of "being the totality," of "being in love," etc., for that necessitates understanding the truth of pure being, the totality, love, which obviously is unknown except when experienced. We cannot designate goals for ourselves of which we know nothing. To do so is wishful thinking. We must start near if we are to go far, we must start with what we are.

CHAPTER 3

Simplicity

Simplicity comes only through self-knowledge, through understanding yourself; the ways of your thinking and feeling, the movements of your thoughts, your responses, your innumerable impediments, attachments, fears, your process of sublimation, substitution, your acquisitiveness, addictions, distractions.

Man, through his constant craving down through the years, has made life a complex and confusing thing. The simple life is belittled, scoffed at, and the possessive, acquisitive life extolled.

More and more things are being urged upon us. Life is becoming more and more complex. And, in order to escape from that we try to renounce, or be detached from things—from cars, from houses, from organizations, from TV, and from the innumerable circumstances outwardly thrust upon us.

Unfortunately, most of you who wish to live simply begin by being simple externally, in outward things. You seem to think that simplicity is an outward expression of withdrawal, having few possessions, wearing a loincloth, having no home, having a small bank account. It is comparatively easy to have few things, to be content with little, and perhaps to share that little with others. But the mere outward expression of simplicity in things, in possessions, does not imply the simplicity of inner being. That comes in the freedom from both possession or nonpossession. It is the indifference to things that comes with deep understanding. Renunciation does not solve the problem.

Most of us live so superficially, on the upper level of our consciousness. There we try to be thoughtful and intelligent, there we try to make our minds simple. Many people practice various disciplines, join various organizations, meditate in a particular fashion, all giving the appearance of simplicity. But the more you suppress, the more you substitute, the more you sublimate, the less there is simplicity. Our minds are so crowded with an infinite knowledge of facts, of what others have said, that we have become incapable of being simple and having direct experience ourselves. It is the simple person who sees more directly, has a more direct experience, not the complex person who may be extraordinarily erudite and clever. Any form of authoritarian compulsion imposed by the government, by family, by yourself, by the ideal of achievement—any form of conformity must make for insensitivity, for not being simple inwardly.

Our problems—social, environmental, political, religious—are so complex that they demand a wholly new approach. There can be a new approach only when you are simple inwardly, really simple. Only when the mind and heart are simple, not encrusted, can you solve the problems that confront you.

You must have the capacity to investigate all things anew; because it is only through direct experience that your problems are solved; and to have direct experience, there must be simplicity, there must be sensitivity.

How to be simple, then, is the problem, because that simplicity makes one more and more sensitive. And a sensitive mind, a sensitive heart is essential. A mind and heart that are not sensitive, not alert, not aware, are incapable of any receptivity, any creative action. If you are not simple you cannot be sensitive to the inward intimation of things.

Simplicity, which is fundamental, real, can only come into being inwardly; and from that there is an outward expression. What you are inwardly affects the outer, overcomes the outer. You come to the inner simplicity by understanding the outer complexity, by finding out how the conflict, the struggle, the pain, exists outwardly. As you investigate more and more you naturally discover the psychological states of your being, the inward complexities, which produce the outer conflicts and miseries. You realize that outward expression is only an indication of your inner state. And in understanding the inner, not exclusively by rejecting the outer, but by understanding the outer and so coming upon the inner—you will find that you become more and more sensitive and free.

Simplicity comes only through self-knowledge, through understanding yourself; the ways of your thinking and feeling, the movements of your thoughts, your responses, your innumerable impediments, attachments, fears, your process of sublimation, substitution, your acquisitiveness, addictions, distractions. You discover how you conform through fear, to public opinion, to what others say, what the Buddha, the Christ, the great saints have said. All this indicates your nature to conform, to be safe, to be secure.

You have to free yourself of all patterns, all beliefs: you must be psychologically free of all things to be simple. That is why it is so important to be aware, to have the capacity to understand the process of your own thinking, to be cognizant of yourself, totally. From that, there comes a simplicity, there comes a humility, which is not a virtue or a practice. It is a state in which you are not important. You look at the problem itself and then you can solve it.

So a religious man is not really one who puts on a robe or a loincloth or lives on one meal a day, or one who has taken innumerable vows to be this and not to be that; but it is he who is inwardly simple, who is not becoming anything. Such a mind is capable of extraordinary receptivity because there is no barrier, there is no fear, there is no going toward something.

True simplicity is love, detached and impersonal, in which there is no longer distinction between the subject and the object. True simplicity is a mind concentrated to the extreme, but absolutely supple, never rigid, always on the alert to grasp the essential. This harmonious whole of love and thought is the simplicity of intuition, which is detachment.

He who has reached true detachment has first freed himself

from the condition of slavery. He is no longer a slave to the causes, which at every moment create a civilization that binds men. He has freed himself. He no longer contributes to the creation of this civilization. His goal is the liberation of man.

You need extraordinary simplicity to understand yourself—the simplicity that comes into being when there is no desire to attain. Simplicity is essential, but it can come into being only when you begin to understand the significances in self-knowledge. The more you understand your process of sublimation, suppression, substitution, the greater the possibility of being simple. The more you free yourself from the innumerable barriers, impediments, fears of the psychological mind, the simpler you will be. Simplicity is a new state of being, in which desire and fear are not present, but in which there is openness, nonresistance and nonprotectiveness. Simplicity can never come from the outside, as a discipline, as an ideal. The more simple you are, the more open you are, the more alert, awake and sensitive you become. Simplicity is the gateway to fact and a primary need of man. Simplicity leads to sensitivity, passive awareness, stillness and spontaneity.

Sensitivity resulting from simplicity does not contain elements of the senses, nor does it contain any functions of psychological thought. Sensitivity begins with simplicity, with the first nonresistant, open recognition of the falsities in your living processes. It is the awakening of a higher faculty. It begins through the presence and significance of fact and increases through greater simplicity, openness, and the constant presence of fact. It is the forerunner of conscious awakening to fact. In the awakened it is the knowing of need, in which there is an ever-increasing awareness and response to the more subtle elements in "what is." Sensitivity determines what is critical in your life. Through it there can be a crisis every moment. Sensitivity determines that which is in the moment.

Your first effort is to sincerely apply yourself. But it is here that lies the initial source of your trouble, and the beginning of the problem of self-consciousness. For actually the only sincerity you know is one that fulfills a self-achieving process, a psychological desire. It is a protective process. What you are sincere about is of primary importance. If you are sincere in self-exposure, then you are open, nonprotective. But most of you use sincerity for gain. In the beginning, when you came to the search for self-knowledge with self-achieving expectancy and sincerely applied yourself, your initial response to it, though unconscious, was obstructive and false. In order to better understand this falsity it will be necessary to consider two psychological elements, expectancy and sincerity.

Expectancy fulfills the purpose of psychological self-protection. It is your constant attitude of mind. With it you meet all experiences in life. Expectancy is the first barrier and screen to understanding, for it is founded upon a vast complex of self-protective conditionings. Expectancy is born of man's psychological motivation for self-continuance, for self-perpetuation. It is founded upon fear and has its roots in gain. Its psychological objective is the constant pursuit of pleasure and avoidance of pain in order to have an inner state of feeling satisfied, assured and comforted. All experiences are met with an attitude of mind of expectant acceptance or rejection, based on expectant profit or loss, expectant success or failure, expectant pain or pleasure. You never do anything without expecting to get something out of it. Thus, you pursue self-knowledge in the same way, hoping to profit from it. In so doing you delude yourself and block the possibility of self-knowledge and understanding.

Sincerity is a manmade moral conceptual quality, which man is supposed to possess or be able to manifest. Sincerity is the moral designation of what man should be, or how he should act when in relationship. Actually, it is an illusory multiple concept, a conglomerate idea consisting of many attributes and qualities, all of which are dualistic in nature, opposites. To be sincere, man must be loyal. He must be genuine, upright, trustful and a host of other attributes and qualities, none of which he really understands.

So to be sincere not only implies how man should conduct himself but how to be several other things as well. It is applied to another desire to gain self-knowledge, in order to gain another something, understanding. Sincerity is self-desire in action for a self-achieving result. It is a complete trap, a circle of reaction within itself, and all that can come out of it will be illusion, manifesting as constant self-contradiction.

You have continued this falsity through the use of the self-achieving moral mechanism. You acted in keeping with what you are, an intellectually conditioned consciousness.

Because of your present manner of thinking and feeling, you do not want to acknowledge fact, need. Your desire-consciousness is directly antagonistic to it, hence immediately sets about to alter, transform, avoid or escape fact. Its purpose is to deny fact, cover it up, for admittance is too painful. It frustrates pleasure fulfillments. Take the case of hunger and food. Man does not use them just for his needs, but utilizes them for social, economic, political, and religious advantages, and self-attainments. From the woman who seeks compliments on her cooking to the use of hunger and food to influence business associates, socially, or for any of the other hundreds of uses made of food, all are psychological devices for the purpose of self-gain, and the denial of need. This holds true for most facts. They are usually twisted and converted into self-satisfactions.

You are in constant contradiction and avoidance of fact. You always avoid being what you are and try to change fact into what you want it to be, into what you think best for yourself. You do not live in fact, in simplicity, but in great complexity. You understand little or nothing, except the satisfaction of desire and escape.

Simplicity is the gateway to fact, and a primary need of man. Simplicity is the open door to sensitivity, spontaneity, passive awareness, and stillness.

CHAPTER 4

Duality

One's experience can open up to you the whole significance of completeness. You must realize inward completeness of being by becoming reflective every moment of the day. Mind in its attempt to get rid of fear cultivates the opposites. The mind divides itself, creates the dual process, a conditioned state, the result of craving.

To understand oneself, consciousness must be studied, not by the present blind acceptance of its processes, its supposed knowledge and values. Instead there must be a total examination of the content of consciousness, its errors and falsities. There must be a complete awakening to them.

This examination should start with an investigation of the outer processes about us, which is our environment, in conjunction with a study of the manner in which man thinks, feels and acts. In our approach there should be a cessation of intellectualizing, the gathering of "information" and "knowledge." Instead, we should observe and question the validity of all values and ideas about us and in us. We must be primarily concerned with the significances and the psychological factors, often deeply hidden, that motivate our behavior in relationship with others and produce our present way of living.

We can know a great deal about life. Our superficial knowledge can be great, can be vast, but this will be only an intellectual concept of life. To have a deep understanding, a deep insight into life, we must first understand that which is taking place about us, and also that which is taking place in us.

In all instances it is necessary to regard that which is perceived as the evidence of what constitutes the consciousness of man. Hence, any approach to the problem of understanding must of necessity be viewed not from the point of view of acquiring knowledge, but as a portrayal and disclosure of the state of consciousness—its processes and function.

The subject matter that follows will present and disclose the substance and significance of the psychological factors and processes of consciousness. For example, if you experience greed, then when such functioning exists in consciousness, at that moment you are greed. The emphasis of understanding is not placed on the object of greed, but on a greedy consciousness, at which time it is greed, for it contains in consciousness both the object and motive of greed. You are in the process of duality.

So, in all that is to follow, try to view it as the portrayal of what is in and of consciousness.

Before you can understand what kind of effort to make in order to know yourself, you must become aware of the kind of effort you are now making. You must understand how thought is putting itself in opposition, this instinctive position as yours and mine, thereby creating duality. It is important to understand this problem of duality as deeply as possible or you will not understand the meaning of conflict, and your efforts to know yourself will be in vain.

Your effort at present consists of escaping from one opposite to another. You live in a series of conflicts of action and response of wanting and not wanting, of becoming and not becoming. You live in a state of duality.

How does this duality arise, this painful conflict between good and bad, hope and fear, love and hate, right and wrong, between the individual and the collective, between the "me" and the "not me"?

The cause of duality is desire, both outgoing desires and desires to reframe. Desire is born of perception, sensation, contact. From these arise experience of either pleasure or pain. If the experience is pleasurable, it creates outgoing desires; if it is painful, it creates restraining desires. The outgoing will or the will to refrain are desires in action. Identity with these two forms of desire creates the "I," causing identification, a difference between you and me, yours and mine and thus the dualistic process comes into being.

That is, through the memory of pleasure and pain in experience, duality is born. This process establishes division and discrimination in consciousness. The thinker is created; fear of repeating the pain or not repeating the pleasure is engendered and the process of continuity is started. Thus the mind is caught up in the past, present and future. It is caught in time.

The dual process is want and not want, expansive desires and refraining desires. The outgoing desires have their own forms of will. The concentration on outgoing desires and their actions creates a world of competition and division, of possessive love and the craving for personal immortality, continuity. Experiencing the pain and sorrow of these outgoing desires, there is the desire to refrain—the other type of will, the will to refrain, to reject, refuse, evade, withdraw, deny, and so on. It is through these two forms of will, of desire, that the thinker sets himself apart from his thought. It is through this dualistic process that man can and does evade what he is, what is actual.

Mind in its attempt to get rid of fear cultivates the opposites. The mind divides itself, creates the dual process, a conditioned state, the result of craving. The mind is caught up in the opposites such as punishment and reward, good and bad, right and wrong, past and future, gain and loss. Thought in the form of the thinker is caught up in this duality and therefore there is incompleteness in action. This incompleteness is the conflict of choice, effort and authority. The escape from the essential to the inessential creates suffering.

Thought divides itself into like and dislike, hate and affection, merit and demerit, the pleasurable and painful, the transient and the permanent, the series of opposites. Our consciousness is the conflict of opposites, of denials and identifications, of the self and the nonself. The content of world consciousness, which we regard as our whole being, is made up of these dual and contradictory values, both mental and emotional. This process, which is the content of consciousness, the unconscious as well as the conscious, we call our own individual mind.

Every day we are confronted with problems, problems which are not theoretical or philosophical but actual. Verbally, emotionally, intellectually, we face them every day; mine and yours, collectivism and individualism, becoming and non-becoming, worldliness and non-worldliness, an endless corridor of opposites in which thought and feelings shuffle back and forth. We are not dealing with this as an abstract, theoretical subject but as an actual problem of our everyday life and conduct. We must become aware that our thought is a constant struggle within the pattern of duality—the good and bad, being and not being, of yours and mine.

These problems of duality, of the opposites, of wanting and not wanting, of becoming and non-becoming, greed and non-greed, war and peace, etc., cannot be solved within the dualistic pattern. Thought must be of a different order to find a permanent answer. There can never be a permanent answer within the conflict of opposites. There can be no integration of the opposites—for example, from greed to non-greed. He who is greedy, though he attempts to become non-greedy, is still greedy. Must he not abandon both greed and non-greed to be of a different order, uninfluenced by either of them? Any becoming involves not becoming. As long as there is the becoming there must be duality with its endless conflict. In duality all relationship is a process of unresolved conflict, of sorrow.

The opposites have a similar common cause. You have to understand them, for all tendencies and virtues hold within themselves their own opposites. To develop an opposite is to escape from actuality. The motive for cultivating the opposite must be understood. If you escape from the struggle and pain of envy and create the opposite, then its opposite becomes identical with itself and so there is no freedom from envy. Whereas if you consider the intrinsic cause of envy, become aware of its various forms, with their urges, then in that understanding there is freedom from envy without creating an opposite.

Generosity, kindliness, love are not opposite to greed, envy, hate. They are of a different order and have nothing to do with contradictions. By putting yourself in opposition to violence, will there be peace? Or is peace something that transcends both the opposites? Virtue is the freedom from the "me" and "mine," the freedom from the conflict of the opposites. In opposites, the real cannot be found. As long as you choose between opposites there is no discernment, and choice and effort are ceaseless and continuous. What is chosen cannot be true. As long as the thinker separates himself from his thought, so long does the vain conflict of the opposites continue.

As long as the thinker is concerned only with the modification of his thought and not with the fundamental transformation of himself, so long will conflict and sorrow continue.

When the thinker and his thoughts are seen to be inseparable, only then is duality transcended. Only then is there the true religious experience. Only when the thinker as a separate entity ceases, when the "I" is not, is there reality.

There is energy, life, unique to each individual. It is not to be qualified or made superintelligent or divine. It is not to be glorified. Through its own self-acting development, it creates its own substance. Through its own ignorance, it is creating for itself limitation and sorrow. There is no question of letting something superintelligent act through its creation, the individual. There is only consciousness as the individual. Consciousness is created through that friction between ignorance, craving and the object of its want.

From this energy, this force, which has become consciousness, there arises the "I" process, the "I" consciousness, the "I" movement. Then the round of creating its own ignorance begins. The "I" process begins and continues in identification with its own self-created limitations. The "I" process always seeks to perpetuate itself. Its action is accumulative craving, ignorance. And that ignorance, like a flame fed by oil, sustains itself through its own activities. That is, the "I" process, the "I," the "I" consciousness, is the outcome of ignorance, and ignorance maintains itself through its own actions of craving and wants. This accumulation and its memories make up the individuality to which you cling and which you crave to immortalize. Can this "I" process, which becomes identified as the "I," be made permanent? Can these accumulations, limitations, be made permanent? Can consciousness, individuality be made permanent? No. Life energy is in a perpetual state of action, movement, in which there can be no individuality. Hence the "I," the "I" process, the "I" consciousness is impermanent.

Most of us have the idea that the "I" is a separate being, something that is enduring. Consciousness itself is the "I." You cannot separate the "I" process from consciousness. There is no "I" that is accumulating experience, which is apart from experience itself. There is only this process, this energy, which is creating its own limitations through its own self-sustained wants.

Our body has its sensations of hearing, seeing, smelling, tasting, feeling. These we shall call sensation. Then there is perception, the power to create images, imagination. All these—body sensation, perception, thought, consciousness, go to create the "I," which in turn creates them.

The "I" is formed through the senses, through emotion, through perception, and from that perception, arises thought, which creates consciousness. Out of this is born separate "I"-ness, which in turn gives birth to self. The "I" does not exist by itself. The "I" is not something that feels by itself; you feel and the "I" is not the "I" that feels and thinks; the "I" is the coordination, the coming together of corporeal existence, which forms the body of sensation, perception, thought, which becomes consciousness. This consciousness, the mind, creates the "I." So you say, "I want to exist. I have a separate existence." So you say, "I think, I feel, I perceive, I am consciousness." But there is no "I." It is but sensation, body perception, thought, consciousness that creates the "I." To keep itself alive, it must believe in its separateness.

The "I" begins to acquire, grasp, hold, and through this grasping, holding, self-consciousness is created, Thus all self-consciousness is acquisition. So the "I" is created in the mind. It does not exist by itself. The "I," the ego, is fabricated by the mind. It is an illusion. It is a bundle of qualities, a center of virtues, sins, ideals. It is a circle in which there is no beginning and no end. Inherently it has no value. It came into being through the lack of understanding. This in turn created conflict, and out of this conflict grew self-consciousness or limited consciousness. This acquiring, grasping "I" thinks that through accumulation it will acquire happiness, completeness. Through the desire for acquisition, it sets up the idea of continuity and the fear of annihilation. So for its well-being, for its maintenance of separateness, it demands the standardization of thought with its implications. It evades all changes. Then there is the standardization of morality, laws to check the "I" from becoming too greedy in acquisition. From this arises fear, the fear of that independent thought, which leads man to become his own law.

Naturally from this there is an erroneous emphasis on individuality, that is; that because you think the individual is separate and the quality of individuality is acquisition, you should emphasize that individuality in acquisition, in work, spiritual attainment, social prestige, in almost everything. You think that through work, through religious ideals, through honors, through possessiveness in relationship, the individual will gain more and more for himself and become more possessive in qualities, friendships and objects.

This is total illusion, for the "I" is itself an illusion. If you base all your civilization, your thought, your culture, your intercourse, your conduct on that illusion, you will not understand truth, you will not live in completeness. You are caught up in the illusion of separateness, which is the cause of sorrow. That limited consciousness, which you call the "I," creates false values, false ideals, self-protective illusions, to all of which the mind becomes a slave.

The "I" consciousness is the action or friction between ignorance and the external provocations of life, of the world. This limited consciousness, this strife and sorrow, is self-perpetuating through want and craving. This in turn creates its own ignorance to which it clings and individualizes.

The limited consciousness is the result of conflict between desire and environment. This consciousness is the result of the various impositions, compulsions to which the mind has submitted itself in its search for security.

The "I," or egotistic consciousness, is made up of these conflicts, compulsions, and the many layers of self-defensive memories.

The outgoing desires and the refraining desires with their various layers of memories, the division between high and low, and the different types of will, form the content of consciousness. So your consciousness—both the conscious and the subconscious—is the repository of ideals, values, images, symbols of the race, of past generations, facts, values, which through time and usage have become pleasant and acceptable. It is composed of ideals, which give you security and comfort, standards of conformity, of thoughts and emotions, which have their origin in fear and primitive reactions. This is the unconsciousness, the mass, of which each one of us is a part whether we know it or not, whether we acknowledge it or not.

With this background the mind lives through an experience and learns from it only further means of self-protection. This limited consciousness having its roots in self-protection cannot evolve, cannot perfect itself. No matter how much it may change, it must ever remain, the center of limitation and frustration, which leads only to illusion.

Our daily thought and action is controlled by the past, by concealed motives, memories, and hidden cravings. In this there is no freedom but only continued imitation caused by fear. Within consciousness there are opposing forces at work, which create duality, want and not want, pain and pleasure, outgoing desires and refraining desires. Instincts, motives, values, prejudices, passions, control consciousness.

If you examine deeply, you will perceive that individuality is a series of accumulative actions, of hindrances, which give to consciousness the identity called the "I." The "I" is a series of memories, tendencies, which are born of craving. If action is the result of prejudice, of fear, of some belief, the action produces limitation. If you have been raised in a particular belief or if you have developed a particular tendency, it must create a resistance against the movement of life. These resistances, these self-protective, egotistic walls of security, give birth to the "I" process.

Consciousness forms its own continuity as an individuality, through the action of resistance and ignorance. It reacts against the actuality of life. It clings with desperate craving to individuality. So individual consciousness, self-consciousness, through reaction to life, opposes, resists the action of life. In this way it maintains limited individuality.

Resistance is the conditioning and limiting of that energy, which may be called life, thought, emotion. This conditioning, the resistance, has had no beginning.

What causes this resistance? We see that resistance can perpetuate itself through acquisitiveness, through conscious and unconscious cravings for experience. It is the perpetuation of conflict. What we call the permanent, this "I"-ness, is part of resistance itself, and so part of conflict. Where there is incompleteness, unfulfillment, there is the craving for continuance, which creates resistance, and this resistance gives to itself the quality of permanency.

All strife is adjustment to two resistances, two individuals. It is only in the state of resistance, of separateness, that there can be the consciousness of relationship. The sense of relationship is but an adjustment between two opposing conflicts. So adjustment between two or more resistances is called relationship. Resistance in relationship is created through accumulated memories; through experience. It becomes more and more strengthened, becoming more and more conscious of itself. It is only in a state of resistance that there can be opposites, conflicts. If you understand this, then you see the problem isn't your resistance in conflict with another but how this resistance came into being and how it is to be dissolved.

The quality of resistance is ignorance, and ignorance is not to be confounded with the mere lack of knowledge. Ignorance is the lack of comprehension of oneself; the unawareness of the process of one's own thoughts and emotions. The "oneself" is not of a given period, and no words can cover the whole process of individuality. Ignorance will exist so long as the mind does not uncover the process of creating its own limitations. We must understand the accumulative process, the craving for identification, the imitation of an ideal, the desire for conformity, continuity. All of this creates authority, engenders fear, leading to delusion. Ignorance is the accumulation of the results of false action.

The individual has not wholly understood the significance of ignorance. We usually try to dissolve or eradicate ignorance of environment, or we try to destroy ignorance through experience. Ignorance cannot be dissolved either through experience or through the control of environment. You must discern how you have come into being, what you are, all the tendencies, reactions, the hidden motives, the self-imposed beliefs and pursuits. Until you understand this, there can be no cessation of sorrow. The confusion of divided action, in economics, in religions, in public and private relationships, will continue. The human problem will disappear only when each one of us is able to discern the self-sustaining process of ignorance. You must come to discern, to realize that you are your consciousness, that you are this process of ignorance, that you made it, you sustain it, and your way of living keeps it alive. If you do not understand your relationship with another and the cause of conflict involved in it, then your relationship with others will inevitably lead to friction and antisocial action. The very comprehension that ignorance is self-sustaining brings that process to an end. It spontaneously, voluntarily withers away if there is that awareness in which there is no desire, no choice.

There are two kinds of experience, that of need and that of wish or want.

The experience based on wish or want is the accumulation of values based on self-protective memories. These values give a mode of behavior that is prompted by personal advantage. Relationship, in this case, is contact between two individualized self-protective memories. It is based on a morality that guards what each possesses. Its reaction is according to conditioned thought and emotion.

What happens when there is experience? It leaves a mark, a scar, on the mind which is memory. With that impression, with that memory, you meet the next experience and from that experience you gather further experience. Each experience leaves its mark on the mind. Now these collective layers of memories, if disagreeable in any way, are essentially based on the desire to protect yourself against further suffering. So you come to an experience already prepared, already protected by your past memories. You are not living completely in that experience, because you have learned how to protect yourself against it, against life. Experience becomes valueless to man who merely uses it as a means of further defense against life.

When you say, "I shall live by my own experiences," you are already placing a limitation on your thought. Although you may say that you are experiencing the actual, you are really experiencing your own wishes. These wishes or wants become so real, so concrete, so definite, that you take them for actuality. This idea that you must live by your own understanding creates complacency. It is ineffectual adjustment leading to stagnation. The use of experience as a means of progress is generally called evolution. You think that through time, this memory, this self-protective record, can reach truth. It cannot. There is no such thing as learning from experience. Yet you are taught that this is the only way you can learn. You are taught that experience is the teacher. This holds true only when you are fulfilling a technique, a pattern which is an imitating action, not a true experience.

Experiences of wish or want are the product of the "I," that consciousness that we call the individuality. The experience of wish or want is the continuance of separative self-consciousness. This kind of experience prevents the comprehension of actuality.

The experience of wish or want must cease in order to experience the actual. True experience is the continual process of releasing the mind from its own limitations. True experience is the breaking down of self-protective walls. It frees the mind, consciousness, of those memories from the past that prevent discernment. If you live in an experience wholly, integrally, without the desire for self-protection, then that experience brings discernment. Truth is realized through the discovery of the true worth of experience. To find that true worth, you must be aware of the essential in each experience. No one can lay down a rule as to which experience will lead to truth and which experience will not. You must discern for yourself the essence of every experience, at all times. If you have the desire to be complete, to experience life itself, then you will not avoid anything through fear; you will try to understand and to assimilate the significance of each experience.

An experience that creates in your mind either great love or a desire for understanding, an experience that shakes the very foundation of your consciousness of individuality, is true experience. One such experience contains the whole significance of life. An experience of love or of death contains the whole of life.

Be aware of all the elements of each experience. Take the experience of love. In that, there is the desire to possess; there is envy, jealousy, loneliness and also the joy of union. By being concentrated, watching all the time, reflecting, you can realize the full significance of that one particular experience, and through it you have understood the whole experience of love.

Or take death. In death is sorrow, pain, frightful loneliness, the desire to be united with the lost one, the desire for sympathy and love. Everyone has it. Instead of gathering the significance of it, the full lesson of it, you seek comfort. The seeking of comfort is the postponement of the liberation of self-consciousness. The struggle to adjust your feeling of loneliness and love in times of death is won by being concentrated, watching all the time, reflecting.

One experience can open up to you the whole significance of completeness. You must realize inward completeness of being by becoming reflective every moment of the day. Don't get lost in sentiment or push all those things of which you are afraid into the background. That completeness, which is in everything, can become real and in that alone there is happiness.

CHAPTER 5

Individuality

The expression of creative intelligence is very rare and though it has the appearance of separative individuality, it is not individuality, but intelligence. When frustration, effort, struggle is present there is the consciousness of individuality. Where true intelligence functions there is no consciousness of individuality.

Individuality is the accumulated and conditioned memories of the past and the present. Each individual is a series of conditioned memories, which impede complete and intelligent adjustment to the living, moving present. These memories give each person the consciousness of separateness, and this is what you call the uniqueness of individuality. Individuality is the full recognition, full consciousness of separate thought, separate emotion, limited and held in the bondage of conditioning and environment:

If you examine deeply, you will perceive that individuality is only a series of limitations, a series of accumulative actions, of hindrances, which give to consciousness the identity called the "I." The individual is the result of the past, expressing himself through the present environment. The "I" is only a series of psychological memories, tendencies, which are born of craving. Action born of the "I" is that friction between craving and its object.

Man prides himself in being individualistic. When you say, "I am an individual," you mean by individuality, the consciousness of separation, and the expression of that consciousness, of that limited thought and of that limited feeling. You call this self-expression.

The individual thinks that by self-expression, through fighting for himself, for his existence, his welfare, he is progressing. You think that through self-expression, through work or art, you will progress toward happiness.

At present, as well as self-expression through individual action in art, writing, music, etc., you have used collective activities to assert your individuality by joining a religious sect, a political party, in social service or by becoming a member of the numberless committees trying to do this or that. You place wrong emphasis on individuality. Individuality cannot be asserted in collective work. It will only produce chaos as it has always done. Reality can never be realized through collective efforts, but only through your own effort. You must do work collectively but seek truth independently, individually.

Brush away all ideals that you have based on the false conception that through spiritual authority, through the effort of another or through an institution or through worship you can realize truth. If you understand this you will plan your life differently. Then there can be no exploitation of others. You will see clearly the difference between the individual's search after reality and collective work. You will plan and work collectively but seek reality individually.

In the vast majority of people, the self-expression of the individual is but the consciousness of separation. What he is engaged in doing is either forced or compelled by circumstances or his own personal wants to take some particular channel of action. What we call individual fulfillment or expression in these cases is nothing but a reaction in which there is very little intelligence.

There is quite a different kind of individuality, that of uniqueness, which is the result of voluntary and comprehensive action. If you understand the environment and act with discerning intelligence, then there is true individuality. This *uniqueness is not separative,* for it is intelligence itself and intelligence cannot be divided into yours and mine. It is only the absence of intelligence that allows the separation of yours and mine, and this is the ugliness of class divisions. Out of these divisions is born exploitation, cruelty and sorrow. The individuality of uniqueness comes when we begin to free ourselves from social influences. This takes place only when the mind sees where the false is, and therefore rejects it. Then only is there an individuality that is not resisting, which is not in opposition to society, an individuality not based on opposition, on resistance, on acquisition. Then the individual has understood the false and has therefore separated himself from it. Only such a being can operate on society, and therefore his responsibility is entirely different. Then he will act, not in terms of disowning or modifying society, but out of his own understanding, his own vitality, which comes through the discovery of that which is false. Then there can be action, which will be effective in the transformation of society, action born of intelligence.

The expression of creative intelligence is very rare and though it has the appearance of separative individuality, it is not individuality, but intelligence. When frustration, effort, struggle are present there is the consciousness of individuality. Where true intelligence functions there is *no* consciousness of individuality.

What is the picture you have of yourself and of the world? The division between you and the world seems actual. Such a division disappears when we examine the individual and the mass. The actual, what is taking place, is the conflict between the individual and the mass. But the individual is the mass and the mass is the individual. The mass is the collective ignorance, want, fear, of individuals. All unexplored regions of consciousness, the half-awakened states of the individual form the mass. This division of the mass and the individual is an illusion. It is creating confusion and misery. You are not completely individual nor are you wholly the mass; you are both the individual and the mass. Individuality ceases, and so does the mass, when the characteristics of the individual, the factors that make up the "I" disappear. It is only when the individual and the mass, as conflicting forces, cease to exist that there is creative intelligence.

CHAPTER 6

Individual and the World

What is needed for true transformation? An inner revolution; a change of consciousness. Transformation is the only solution to the present critical state of the world. Love is the only thing that transforms. There is only one problem; it is a lack of love. This is the element that is missing in all of us.

We must become aware of the gravity of the present structure of society. Politically there is dissension, deceit, distrust, confusion and uncertainty throughout the world. Morally human relationships have become dull, insensitive, self-centered, greedy, whether considered from the individual or national point of view. Social life has become the mad pursuit of distraction, escape, amusement and sensation. Religions have proven themselves inadequate to solve man's problems. They have not changed man but have only added to the confusion and divisions. Education has not enlightened man but addresses itself to the pursuit of self-achievement. Economic greed, the possession and control of things, has become the dominant motive of the individual and the many. Wars and the preparations for destruction have increased throughout the world.

The crisis today is extraordinary and we are trying to solve it by formulas. The socialist feels with his formula the problem will be solved. This is true of the communist, capitalist, the organized religionist, the fascist. The left and the right are trying to find solutions through formulas, certain set ideas. But systems have never solved anything nor have they brought about any fundamental change.

Many people think that through legislation, through organization or through a leader the problems of war and peace and other human problems will end. Some think that if only things were well organized so that all could have enough of everything the world would be happy and peaceful. But this would not be so if individually we have not understood our desire to possess and dominate. Even with a fair distribution of things, however necessary, this desire to possess and dominate will lead to conflict and hatred. Outward change, however beneficial or utilitarian, is of little use. It is the inner that overcomes the outer, not the outer that fulfills the inner.

You say that more emphasis should be laid on changing social organizations. But the problems of confusion and conflict existing in the world today are the result of the manner in which man thinks, feels and acts. He created these problems, this confusion, these conflicts. He is entirely responsible for his relationship with the one and the many.

Man's present purposes and methods of fulfillment, his method of thinking, feeling and acting is limited and erroneous when it defeats peace and unity. It constantly creates and expresses itself through conflicting issues. Man's acting, thinking and feeling have created racial hatreds, religious prejudice, class-consciousness, economic exploitation, military destruction and suppression, political domination and control.

We all see the necessity, the importance of social change. Wars, starvation, ruthless pursuit of power, and so on—with these we are familiar. And you earnestly desire to change these conditions. You want to bring order in society, but how are you going to do it?

As of now, the clever ones, the political leaders, the social and economic experts, the organized religionists, the educators, the psychologists, the philosophers have not solved any of our human problems. Intellectually we have many theories of how our problems could be solved. Politically we are offered certain patterns either through compulsion and conformity or by accepting a certain set of ideas; and the religionists throughout the world offer hope, either in the future or through living according to certain patterns laid down by the teachers. Scholastically, the educators, the psychologists, the philosophers offer their special ways and means of solving our human problems. Social leaders offer adjustments within their particular field, and economic experts claim the solution lies in the proper production and distribution of things. Repeatedly we have tried the solutions put forth by the experts, but all have resulted in failure. We have only moved further away from the solution of our problem, this destructive complexity of living with its constantly increasing confusion and conflict.

What has happened? Why did this come about?

This has come about because we fulfill our lives through comparative, psychological change. Change in thinking, as we know it, implies comparative change, modified continuity—a different form of the same thing. It is a change from this to that. The society is this and I want it to be changed to that. The individual is this and he wants to be changed to that. When we want a change, an individual change or a social change, it implies a change toward something that we already know. We know the change we are hoping for. Leftists, Marxists, regard revolution as the necessary outward transformation. All idealists and searchers for truth regard transformation as coming from an inner conformity to the methods laid down by religious teachers. This is a modification of continuity, which implies an adjustment to a preconceived pattern that needs adjustment. Every social or individual change is only modified continuity of what already exists. When one thinks of changing society, such a change will only be a modification of what is already there, no matter how violent the modification may appear. When one thinks of change in an individual through conformity to a pattern, such change will be but a modification however sanctimonious it may seem. This is what is taking place in the world, in the lives of people. The opposite is invariably the continuity of the same thing in a different form. Whether political, idealistic or otherwise. When we deliberately set about to change the present system in regard to outer conditions, is not all such change the same thing continued in another form? When the individual deliberately sets about to change his way of living, does he not choose that way which appeals to him? Such choice is a change continued in the same form. We want a continuity of what we like and a discontinuity of what we do not like.

When we talk about social or individual revolution, we have to understand what is meant by "change." How can the "known" change except into a further "known"? So, whatever changes we may undergo through our present form of thinking and feeling will only be a change in thinking, a change within the same psychological field, not a real change of thinking. And a change within the same field cannot change that which exists, it can only modify it and thus add to the complexity and confusion.

Because we do not understand this everyday existence with its conflicts and complexities, we use ideas, explanations, authorities to remove uncertainty and suffering and to establish permanence and security. If you consider your thoughts and the acts springing from them, you will see that where there is a desire to escape a given situation it comes from the search for security. Because you find conflict in life, with all its actions, its affections, its thoughts, you want to escape to a satisfactory security. So your whole action is based on this desire for security, for permanency, for outer and inner conditions adequate to give and maintain certainty. Your mind is caught up in a constant clinging to that which gives satisfaction and comfort.

Through this search for security you have created in you a state of permanency, an "I," an identity that you consider to be real. This sense of "I" gives rise to conflict between that "I," which you assume to be permanent, and the movement of life, which is ever-changing. So conflict exists between the changing values of life and your desire for permanency.

What then is this "I" that has assumed permanency and is ever seeking further continuity? You cannot intelligently examine this question until you understand your present critical capacity.

This critical capacity springs from your accumulated prejudices, beliefs, theories, hopes or from what you call experience. Experience is based on tradition, on accumulated memories. Your experience is always tinged by the past, by your conditioning. A conditioned mind acting in a conditioned way cannot experience anything new. Such a mind is incapable of fully experiencing the reality or non-reality of things. Likewise a mind that is already prejudiced by a conscious or unconscious desire for permanence cannot fully comprehend the truth, reality. To such a prejudiced mind all inquiry merely strengthens your existing prejudice.

The search and longing for security and permanency, for immortality, is the urge of accumulated memories of individual consciousness, the "I," with its fears and hopes, loves and hates. This "I" breaks itself into many conflicting parts—the higher and the lower, the permanent and the transient, the good and the bad, and so on. The "I" in its desire to perpetuate itself, seeks and uses many ways and means to entrench itself.

Your mind is continually seeking new substitutes, other ideas and beliefs, hoping for security and happiness. It goes from one hope to another, from one illusion to another, from one belief to another. You are accustomed to systems, to philosophies, to concrete ideas in which your thought can carefully wrap itself, and you call this living. You invent a lot of theories and speculations, join various groups, follow teachers and masters, perform rituals, gather into little cliques, quote authorities, join organizations, imitate the great, gather ideas, things, people and feel superior to others—but all this leads nowhere. They are merely the immature actions of thoughtless people.

You spend your time looking for a descriptive explanation of truth instead of trying to find out how you can realize it. Most people have read, listened and imitated; have tried to find out what others have said about truth and God, about life and immortality. They have a picture in their mind and they will compare that picture with this which they are reading. But here there will be no attempt to describe truth, for it cannot be described, so naturally there will be confusion in the reader's mind.

If you really probe into your own minds and hearts, you will discover that you are trying to get something new, a new idea, a new sensation, a new explanation of life in order that you may mold your own life to that. Therefore you are seeking a satisfactory explanation. You are searching for certainty—certainty of knowledge, certainty of truth, certainty of an idea—in order to be able to act with certainty. In searching out various kinds of gain, in seeking authorities that give security and comfort, in striving for development of character—through all these attempts you hope to have assurance of certainty that takes away all doubts and anxiety. You make life into a school where you learn to be certain.

But life is not a process of gathering in. Life is to be lived naturally, fully, without this constant battle of conflicts, this distinction between the essential and the inessential. From this idea of life as a school where you learn to be certain, there arises the constant desire to find ultimate truth, God the final perfection, which you hope will give you that certainty. Hence your continual attempts to adjust to social conditions and the cultivation of virtues. These standards and demands, if you really think about them, are shelters from which you act, shelters to establish a sense of permanency. When you seek a master, a teacher, an authority, you are seeking a certainty to which the mind can cling, in which the mind can feel safe, secure.

What happens when you are following an authority, religious or otherwise? You are being standardized; you need only conform. Thus you need not think at all, you need not go through conflict. Instead you take an idea, which another has thought out, lived, struggled with, given his life to understand, and you mold your life according to that pattern. But if you really understand this, you will see that you cannot have a standard or a system, either external or your own, and that this search for security is but an escape from conflict. If you conform to a pattern your life will become a standardized emptiness. That is what happens to people who are seeking a conclusion, an end, who are looking to another for guidance.

Since you as an individual are confused, you are bound to spread confusion. Your state, your government, your religion, each one of these is bound to be confused because you are in that state, and you bring about your society. Society is the relationship between two or more individuals. The society around you is the extension of yourself. Your greed, your hate, your fears are projected in action into the world—so it is we ourselves who create the world crisis.

War is the outward and spectacular result of our daily life. If we do not transform our daily life and bear responsibility for it, not superficially but profoundly, we and the society we have created cannot escape from the catastrophe that is coming. Therefore the individual is all important, not as the individual in opposition to society, in opposition to the whole. We must be very clear about this point. When we regard the individual and his function in society, we have to consider the individual as a whole. Let us not put the individual in opposition to the mass. They are not different. You, the individual, are the mass, the result, the mass. You will discover, if you go into it deeply, that you are both the many and the particular. You are the product of your background, of your tradition, of your environmental influences, of your religious training. We are the result of everything about us, and the things about us are in turn created by us. The society that exists about us at the present time is the product of our desires, of our responses, of our thoughts and actions. We project the society and then become the instrument of that society. You are the product of the society, which you yourself have created. There is no division between the individual and society.

You may have a particular name, own a piece of land, a private house, have personal relationships, a separate bank account. Though all this makes you think you are separate, you are a part of the whole. After all, your mind is the result of the past, both the conscious and the unconscious. It is the result of thoughts, efforts, struggles, intentions and desires of all human beings. You are the sum total of the entire human struggle. You desire alike, you think alike, are conditioned alike. So the society and the individual are alike. Society and the individual are one.

The division between the mass and you, the individual, creates confusion and conflict, ruthlessness and misery. If you can understand that the individual, the you, is part of the whole, not only mystically but actually, then you will free yourselves happily and spontaneously from the greater part of the desire to compete, to succeed, to oppress, to be ruthless, or to become a follower or a leader. Then you will regard the problem of existence quite differently. It is important to understand this deeply. As long as you regard yourself as an individual apart from the whole, competing, obstructing, opposing, sacrificing the many for the particular or the particular for the many, all those problems that arise of this conflicting antagonism will have no solution. The catastrophe we face has been brought about by each one of us. We are confused within ourselves and that confusion manifests itself in the outer. So each one—Muslim, Hindu, Christian—is responsible for our appalling crisis, the crisis of human survival. Neither the capitalist, communist, nor the socialist can escape it. We are all responsible and must confront it. That is what is meant by bringing about a new way of looking at life; and therefore it is important to realize how extraordinarily important the individual is at the present time.

We must differentiate between the individual and individualistic action. Individualistic action takes place when the individual acts as separate from the whole. When he is thinking in terms of himself, his power, his reputation, his career, his position—then he is acting individualistically. This is how resistance against another is created, and that resistance through accumulative memories, through experience, through conditioning, through our present process of thinking and feeling, is more and more strengthened, becoming more and more conscious of itself. If we do understand this, then we see the problem is not that of one resistance against another, but how this resistance comes into being and how it is to be solved.

When you see that the world is about to be blasted by bombs and feel the horror of it; when the world is broken up by separate religions, competing nationalities, races, ideologies, what is your answer? Will you just go on living briefly and dying and hope that some good will come of it? Mankind is ourselves, you and me. Where does the solution lie except in ourselves? To discover the real answer requires deep thought-feeling and few of us are willing to go deeply enough. If each one of us considers this problem as springing from within himself and is not willing merely to be driven helplessly along in this appalling confusion and misery, then we shall find a simple and direct answer.

What is required at the present time is not a new formula, not a new system either of the left or the right, but a wholly different approach. This is important. If you have a problem, what matters is how you approach it. If you approach it with a fixed mentality, with set ideas, you will not solve the problem because the problem is not static. It is constantly changing and it cannot be solved by formulas. So the approach to the problem is all important. The how is more important than the "action." So to know how to approach the catastrophe that faces mankind is more important than what to do about it. That "how" can only be understood when we are capable of looking at the problem through ourselves and not through any formula. It is a world catastrophe. It requires a mind that is capable of looking at it without any prejudice. You cannot look at it as a Brahmin or as a Buddhist or as a Christian. You cannot look at it as a capitalist or as a communist or as a socialist. Because we have looked at it in the past in this way we have brought about this problem and if we approach the problem with the same mentality, we shall not clarify or understand it, but only further it. We are standing at the edge of a precipice with our minds closed, biased, a bias created by centuries of division.

If we really want to understand this crisis we must abandon the causes that have brought us to this stage and look at the problem. But here is where our difficulty lies, for we can only understand the problem by understanding ourselves. We know the catastrophe, we know the sociological causes of the wars that have been fought.

Preparations are going on with marvelous skill for another war and you and I know that this is the edge of the precipice. We read about it but we are distracted from the issue by our immediate demands, pleasures and pains. But the catastrophe is enormously serious and that is why, if we would salvage something out of this catastrophe, we must become serious. If the problem was serious enough to us we would do something about it. It is not sufficiently immediate. We are looking to leaders, to gurus, teachers, formulas, systems. But we are at the very edge of it and we have to confront it. Each one of us has to solve this problem and not leave it to others or to the leaders.

The problem, this catastrophe, requires not static thinking but revolutionary thinking, a thinking that is not based on any ideology, whether Hinduism, Christianism, nationalism, communism, capitalism, socialism. It requires a change of thinking not a change in thinking. We must feel the whole picture and not just a part of it. Our difficulty is to feel the whole rather than the particular. At present we look at the problem through our own country, our own ideas, our way of doing things. We are not able to perceive the extent of the problem because of our opinions about ourselves, our fears, beliefs, hopes, traditions. We are surrounded by the immediate, the national, our own way of fulfilling life. To understand the whole picture of this catastrophe that exists around us, wars, famines, death, insecurity, disillusionment, there must be a fundamental change of thinking.

Fundamental change is the living quality of life. Everything around us and in us is in constant change, becoming and decaying. All things become worn out by use, there is nothing permanent. In our institutions, our theories of government, of economics, of social relationships—in all things there is flux, there is constant change. The manifestation of constant change gives evidence that there is nothing permanent to which the mind can attach itself. If this is so, there can be no personal center that is gathering to itself experiences, lessons for the future. There is an intellect, which can, does and should acquire knowledge of the physical, factual world. But there is no separate entity, no center that can gather subjective experiences, qualities, virtues for future use and protection. This is simply the intellect playing a double role. Acquiring knowledge of the world is its true function. All the other is a false psychological use of the mind. We must understand this integrally, not merely superficially, intellectually. We must use the correct function of the mind if we are to fundamentally alter our relationship with the one and the many, which is now based on ignorance, fear, wants, not wants—the false psychological, intellectual process. If you can feel deeply and become aware that all things are in a state of continuous change, constantly becoming, then you will be able to free yourself from this conflict that exists in yourself and so in your neighbor and in society. Intellectually you may grasp this, but emotionally each one clings to a personal, static center, identifying himself with it. Conflict must inevitably arise when there is a static center, the "I" within us, while all about us there are changing values. Our attachment to what we consider to be a permanent center indicates that we are in resistance to the constant movement of life.

If we deeply understand the importance of ourselves and of the things of this world, then there will be no attachment to ideas, things or people, from which arises the social and individual struggle. It is necessary for us to clearly understand that for a fundamental change of thinking to take place, mind cannot be in bondage to things, ideas and people. If you are seeking reality, that essence of life in which all sense of individualism has wholly ceased, you cannot imitate any person, rely on learning, follow any system. You cannot be controlled, dominated and influenced by things, ideas or people.

If you are caught up in the bondage to an idea you can never understand truth, because you are in continuous self-limitation. You will never experience a fundamental change of thinking by trying to become something through an idea or through knowledge.

What then is to be done?

What is needed is transformation, an inner revolution, a change of consciousness. Transformation is the only solution to the present critical state of the world. Love is the only thing that transforms. There is only one problem; it is the lack of love. That is the element that is missing in all of us. Therefore there is no communion between us, but only verbal relationship. We are on the edge of things, not in the center. Because there is no affection, which means love, there is no understanding.

Love is present when there is total responsibility. Then one is transformed. And through transformation, we will find that love has no individual relationship; it is neither personal nor impersonal. In love there is no "I," no self, no emotion, sentiment, devotion. There is no gratification in love. In it there is no friction, no resistance, but a state of complete integration. Love cannot be brought into being through discipline, through any means, through any intellectual urgency. Love has no frontiers, it has no class, no race, no color. It is a state of being, which comes when the activities of the self have ceased. Love is the freedom from violence, craving, vanity and greed. Love is the acceptance of the actual and therefore of the real.

Transformation is creative activity, the meeting of the new as the new, without any conditions, without any of the psychological process of thinking and feeling. You meet the new with the new. Transformation is a complete alteration in direction. It is rebirth, a new state of being, a new state of consciousness.

The classical understanding of transformation is when the "me," the "I," is driven out never to return. This is false, for when transformation has taken place, the "I" has simply disappeared, dropped away. Any attempt to "drive out" or be free of the "I," the "me," is false effort. Transformation comes when one's approach and action is not to get anything or be rid of anything, but to perceive and understand the cause of that which is about us and in us. The problem is not that "I must transform myself" or "drive out" the "I." Transformation cannot be achieved, it must take place. It cannot take place while looking for a result or searching for security. But looking at the new anew is an action devoid of protection in which one is in direct response to life, the actual.

To experience the real, there must be a state of experiencing. It is only in the state of experiencing, when there is neither the experiencer nor the experience, that there is instant transformation. If you understand the "what is" of the moment completely, then a "miracle" happens. Transformation is not a matter of words and explanations; it comes instantaneously when we see things clearly. We can keep our minds fresh and new only by constantly experiencing. Transformation is not a static state; it is the essence of constant change, life, and in the constant change of life it must be continuously fulfilled. There are no tricks, no bypaths, there is no golden key that unlocks the door to understanding. Only you and you alone must meet the issues of life and understand them.

Transformation must always be immediate and not left to time consciousness. We must understand now, from moment to moment.

Understanding is always in the now and not in the tomorrow. And the now is an experience in consciousness of the real, of the moment. Any postponement is not conducive to transformation, to understanding. Transformation is entirely different, quite a different process than that of modified continuity, which is our present way of thinking and feeling, the intellectual process. Hence transformation is possible only through understanding in the now.

Can an individual transform himself or another?

When the individual attempts to change (change being only modified continuity), whatever the individual creates will be only a modification of what he already is. If the relationship between two individuals is mere static adjustment, it produces a society that is static. If the relationship is revolutionary, based on a different sense of values, then the relationship will be creative. Therefore continuous revolution, transformation, is in relationship with people. Therefore you must start with yourself and not with society.

Societies may appear to have been in a state of revolution but history has shown that these revolutions are only modifications and the same problems as before soon manifest themselves. An individual alone can be in a state of revolution, but not society.

So individual transformation is the only solution to the world chaos. You can only do something for the world in which you live by transforming yourself. Individual transformation alone will lead other individuals to transform themselves, and this will bring about a revolution in thought and therefore in action. Only when the individual transforms himself is there the possibility of revolution, the transformation, the regeneration of the world.

War with its miseries, the limitation of national frontiers, the economic situation, the disintegration of society, the helplessness of religions, the confusion of political leaders—these vast complexities make you feel frustrated with the enormity of the problem. But frustration is a false response. You are not called upon to deal with the problems of the world. You may talk about them, you may rebel against atom bombs, you may gossip about what others say about them. But you cannot do anything about them. They are not your problem.

First you must see that you cannot do anything about all this. The confusion is so colossal that your individual acts can obviously do nothing. You cannot persuade the leaders to do what you think is correct. You cannot prevent the world and the people from going their own way. It is not possible for you to change all this. To participate in it is only to continue and further it. Only through individual regeneration, transformation, can a fundamental change come about.

Knowing the truth of this, you should not attempt to solve the problems of the world. Recognize that immediate transformation is the only solution. So far you have been contributing to the confusion and chaos in the world; now you will change your focus and start with yourself. But not in withdrawal, not in isolation, but to find the actual. An individual can create a structure away from all this confusion. You see the importance of immediate transformation, not in terms of time, but of complete regeneration of thought, clarity, creativeness. Then you will transform yourself. To do this you must have complete transformation now, transformation in values, in outlook and in your whole being. You must leave your present way of life, your ideals, formulas, standards, organizations, systems, etc., and become reborn. Your present mechanical form of living with its mechanical intellect must be discerned and transcended. The studied, planned, disciplined, patterned life must cease. To be made anew through formulas, beliefs, by the mechanical intellect with its complexities and anxieties, is absurd. You must examine the causes of the present chaos, find out what is distraction, what is false, and what leads to transformation. When you know and understand the movement of life, then life will have a meaning; you will be purposeful and proceed directly.

It must be understood that a wide gap exists between our present everyday life and the pursuit of the real, the actual. The gap exists because change involves not only physical comfort but a painful realization of one's insensitivity, one's incapacity. It will create uncertainty, and you dislike being uncertain. This gap can be bridged only when you see the absolute necessity for the cessation of all psychological, intellectual escapes and the need for integral action, understanding, out of which is born true relationship.

Life is, and must be, a series of challenges and responses. The challenges are not according to your likes and dislikes, not according to your particular desires, but assume different forms at different times. If you have the capacity to meet these challenges adequately, fully, directly, you will find there is no problem.

So to bring about in each of us the capacity to discover what is true, becomes essential, for to discover truth is liberating, creative. It is the lack of this capacity that creates problems. When we have that capacity, then the problem ceases to exist. It is the incapacity to understand a challenge that brings about problems.

So how are we to bring about that capacity to meet the challenge? How is one to have that capacity, how does one come by it?

No information can give it. Though you may study all the books written about how to meet life, that form of understanding is an impediment. Because having the facts, you try to meet the challenge with that framework of information. Intellectual knowledge does not bring about capacity. It is not acquired facts, it is not acquired knowledge that will help you to have that capacity with which to meet life.

Before you can find out if it is possible for you to have the capacity to meet life fully, directly, you must discover what life itself is. What is living? If you can understand that, you will have the capacity to meet the challenge, which is life itself. Life is experience, experience in relationship. So in understanding relationship we shall have the capacity to meet life fully, adequately. Our problem is not inherent capacity, a talent, a gift. Capacity is not independent of relationship, but rather the understanding of my relationship with another. This understanding naturally produces the capacity for quick pliability, for quick adjustment, for quick response. The capacity to understand comes into being only when one understands relationship. Capacity comes with self-knowledge.

To understand yourself requires objective, kindly, dispassionate study of yourself, yourself being the organism as a whole—your body, your feelings, your thoughts. They are not separate, they are interrelated. It is only when you understand the organism as a whole that you can go beyond and discover still further, greater, vaster things. But without this primary understanding, without laying a tight foundation for right thinking, you cannot proceed. If you do not understand yourself, you will not understand anything else. We may have great ideas, beliefs and formulas, but they will have no reality. They will be delusions. We must understand ourselves to understand the present and through the present the past. From the known present, the hidden layers of the past are discovered and this discovery is liberating. We must lay the right foundations for right endeavor. The right means lead to right ends and wrong means will produce wrong ends.

Right endeavor is the first task, even before the problems of war and peace, of economic and social conflicts, of death and immortality. These questions will arise, they are bound to arise, but in discovering ourselves, in understanding ourselves, the questions will be rightly answered. So if we are really serious about these matters, we must begin with ourselves in order to understand the world of which we are a part. Without understanding ourselves, we cannot understand the whole, because whatever the problems; they are projected by us. We are the world. We are not independent of the world. The world's problems are our own. To understand the problems around us, which are the projections of ourselves, we have to understand ourselves in relationship to everything. And there cannot be understanding if we begin by comparing, condemning, justifying. It is the nature of the mind to condemn, to justify, to compare. You see in the mirror of relationship your own reactions and idiosyncrasies; how your instinctive response is to justify or condemn your reactions. The understanding of the process of your thinking, this process of comparison, of condemnation and justification, is the beginning of self-knowledge and right thinking. Without self-knowledge you cannot go very far.

Self-knowledge is realized through your search of yourself. To realize self-knowledge is arduous. The beginning and the end is in you. Without knowing yourself, what you think and what you feel will be erroneous. The root of all understanding lies in understanding yourself. When you find out the cause of your thought-feelings, from that discovery you will know how to think-feel. Then there is the beginning of understanding. Without knowing yourself, the accumulation of ideas, the acceptance of beliefs and theories has no basis. Without knowing yourself you will be caught in uncertainty, depending on moods, on circumstances. Without knowing yourself, you cannot think rightly. If I do not know my motives, intentions, my background, my private thought-feelings, how can I agree or disagree with another or know what is true? How can I establish a true relationship with another? How can I discover anything of life if I do not know myself? Right thinking is not to be discovered through books or merely listening to some people's ideas of what right thinking is. Right thinking is to be discovered for yourself, through yourself.

There can be peace and happiness in the world only when the individual—who is the world—alters the causes within himself, which produce confusion, sorrow, hate, war. Then there will be creative living with the one and the many.

CHAPTER 7

Authority

Dependence on authority prevents your understanding of any problem. Every problem is a new problem. Problems are invariably self-induced; therefore it is important to understand the whole process of yourself without authority, without following a pattern or looking up to an example, an ideal, or a leader. Self-knowledge is the beginning of the end of all conflict, and it is only when conflict ceases that there can be creative living.

Environment consists of that which is about us, both the actual and the psychological, and that which is in us, both the actual and the psychological. It consists of such illusions as authority, imitativeness, beliefs, ideals, opinions. These illusions have developed a consciousness, which maintains and demands individualized action, which keeps man in conflict with this environment, with ideas, things and people.

The difficulty with us is that our thinking is conditioned. We may be French, or English, or German, or Hindu. We have our particular religious, political, social, educational and economic backgrounds, and through this screen of this psychological environment we try to *meet* the problems of life, and thereby increase our problems. We do not meet life without conditioning; we meet it as an entity with a particular training, with a particular background, experience.

Being conditioned, you meet life according to your particular patterns, with your particular beliefs, ideas, ideals, knowledge, and processes of living. This reaction, according to pattern, only creates more problems. Obviously, then, you have to understand and remove these conditionings, which increase your problems. Most of us are unaware that we are conditioned, that our conditioning is the result of our own background and our own desire, our own longing for security. After all, the society about us is the outcome of our desire to be secure, to be safe, to be permanent in our own particular form of conditioning. Being unaware of our conditioning, we continue to create more problems. We have such an accumulation of knowledge, so many prejudices, so many ideologies, so many beliefs, to which we cling. These backgrounds, these conditionings, prevent us from actually meeting life as it is. We are always meeting life, which is a challenge, with our inadequate responses, and so never understand life, except through our particular conditionings. The challenge of life is in constant transformation, in constant flux. We must understand not the challenge, but our reaction to it.

Our concern should be with this inner and outer environment, not with the conflict, not how to overcome the conflict, not how to run away from it. By questioning the environment and trying to understand its significance, we shall find out its true worth. We are enmeshed, caught up in the process of trying to overcome, to run away from circumstances, environment. We are not trying to find out what it means, what is its cause, its significance, its value.

When are you conscious of environment? Only when there is conflict and resistance to that environment. So if you observe, if you look at your life, you will see that conflict is continually twisting, perverting, shaping your life; and intelligence, which is mind and heart, has very little part in your life. That is, environment, which is authority, is continually shaping, molding, your life and action. Naturally out of continual twisting, molding, shaping, perversion, conflict is born.

Conflict can only exist between two false things, between that supposed reality you call the "I" and the environment itself. Your mind is merely concerned with the overcoming of that struggle. If you understand the significance of environment, wealth, poverty, exploitation, oppression, nationalities, religions, and all the inanities of social life, not trying to overcome them but seeing their significances, then there must be individual action, and complete revolution of ideas and thought.

Due to uncertainty, man ever seeks certainty and accepts the authorized statements of those who promise him fulfillment of his craving. We crave for certainty, but this craving creates ignorance and illusion. It establishes psychological instruments of faith and authorities who will reward and punish.

Authority is the greatest hindrance to the flow of life. It is one of the most destructive barriers. We have created authorities in our desire for self-protection and security.

For convenience let us here divide authority into the outer and inner. The outer authority is environment, habit, tradition, knowledge, the closed morality of religion, the authority of experts, and the authority of vested interests. The inner authority is the result of our reactions to this compulsion from without. This inner authority develops an inner law based on fear, on the self-protective memory of security, and comfort. These are the subtle subjective authorities of accumulative memories, prejudices, antipathies, fears, wants, hopes, which have become values, ideals, standards. According to them we are continually adjusting and paralleling our conduct. These in their own subtle way control and limit thought and action and thus create their own conflict and suffering.

If you examine the activity of the mind, you will see that it is constantly accepting and rejecting authority. It is constantly conditioning itself by new values and standards. Authority, whether objective or subjective, is the same, because authority implies shaping, and imitation, a control, a conditioning, whether imposed externally or by inward effort and exertion. Authority is the first hindrance, a process of imitation, falseness. Authority makes man into an imitative machine, into a cog—whether in a social or a religious machine.

You can find out how to live intelligently only when you understand environment, which is creating conflict and mere substitutions. If you desire to understand environment, authority, not only the objective but the subjective, which is infinitely subtle, then you must individually come into conflict with it. It is only when in conflict, in suffering, that you, the individual, begin to discover the true significance of values. As most people are afraid to come into contact with conflict, suffering, they only intellectually perceive the significance of authority, environment. So they leave the responsibility of action to the mass, the vague and unreal entity, which they hope will miraculously alter their environment, and so bring happiness to them.

To understand the cause of authority, you must follow the mental and emotional process which creates it. First of all, you feel empty, inadequate, and in order to get rid of that feeling you make an effort. By that effort you create opposites, what you are and what you think you should be. You create a duality, which only increases your sense of incompleteness and emptiness.

If you could find a way out of your conflict you would not take recourse to authority. You turn either to inner or outer authority for guidance and comfort. So, authority becomes very important in your life. Because you are unable to understand and resolve conflict, you use authority as a means of avoiding conflict; and the means then becomes all important, and not the fathoming, the exploring of the process of conflict itself.

So you have authorities of innumerable kinds, inner as well as outer. Outer authority takes the form of knowledge, examples, teachers, and so on, and inner authority is based on your own experiences and memories to which you turn for guidance in moments of conflict and anxiety. Authority, both outer and inner, offers hope.

But can authority of any kind, inner or outer, resolve your problems? The more you seek authorities, ideals, conclusions, hopes, the more you depend on them; and dependence on authority becomes much more significant than the understanding of the conflict itself. The more you depend on authority, the more dependent you become, and dependence ultimately destroys confidence in your own understanding. You have no confidence in your own capacity to find out, to explore.

Confidence is not arrogance. But for some people the more they are experienced, the more they are inwardly certain, the more arrogant and obstinate they become. Such self-confidence is only self-enclosure, a process of resistance.

But there is a different kind of confidence, which is not arrogance, not cumulative. To explore into the nature of conflict, you cannot bring to it that which you have accumulated; if you explore with previous knowledge, it ceases to be exploration. Then you are merely moving from the known to the known, from certainty to certainty, from what you have experienced to what you hope to experience. That is not exploration. That is merely the cumulative process of knowledge, of experience, and the confidence it brings is assertive arrogance.

However, there is a confidence which is subtle, worthwhile, and which comes when there is no sense of accumulation of any kind, but a constant exploration and discovery. This creates no arrogance. It is this state of constant discovery, the capacity for constant exploration, that brings about enduring confidence, which is not arrogance. And that confidence, which is so essential, is denied when there is authority of any kind, when you depend on or look up to another for guidance in conduct. When you are dependent, it does give a certain self-assurance, even though it entails fear. But that assurance of following someone, belonging to a group, believing in an idea or in certain dogmas, is a self-enclosing process.

The mind that is constantly isolating itself is bound to awaken fear. And in that fear you go from one authority to another, from one emotional experience to another. In this process, problems are never resolved. They only multiply.

Is it possible to look at our conflicts without bringing in any authority, external or internal? You can be passively aware of conflict without the choice of condemnation; that is, you can be aware, not as the observer observing your experience or analyzing the thing in yourself that you wish to destroy, but aware with that passivity in which the observer is the observed. In that state of mind you will see that the problems are understood and resolved. But if you choose the way of action with regard to a problem, compare or condemn it, you only increase resistance, and therefore multiply the problem. The multiplication of problems comes into being only when you seek an answer, a conclusion, and so depend on an authority, outer or inner. Dependence on authority actually prevents your understanding of any problem. Every problem is a new problem. Problems are invariably self-induced; therefore it is important to understand the whole process of yourself without authority, without following a pattern or looking up to an example, an ideal, or a leader. Self-knowledge is the beginning of the end of all conflict, and it is only when conflict ceases that there can be creative living.

CHAPTER 8

Mind

The mind, which is intelligent, does not seek security.
It reveals to itself its own fears and wants.
Out of this arises integral awareness of its impermanency.
This recognition alone can set the mind free
from its self-created bondage.

Psychological mind is the result of the past. What you and I are is the outcome of many yesterdays. We are the total summation of the past and without understanding that past we cannot proceed.

Our conditioning is the mind; the mind is the seat of all conditioning, conditioning being knowledge, experience, identification with a particular party, with family, with a particular race, group or nation; it is tradition, ideas, beliefs, conclusions, opinions, theories, facts. Mind is the entire memory, both of the past and the present. It is speech, consideration and understanding. Essentially psychological mind is sentiment, disposition, like and dislike, want and not want, thought and feeling, possessive love, fear. Mind is the intellect with all its faculties. It is the comparative process of thinking. The intellect and its faculties enables the mind to receive, revive or modify perceptions, conceptions and conclusions. Mind is all states, relations and functions of psychological consciousness.

The mind is ever perplexed by conflict and constant change, so it seeks finality, deep assurance, a changeless state. It seeks comfort, consolation, certainty and continuity. Mind, as we know it, is an instrument developed for survival, for satisfaction, for self-protection, for resistance and therefore is an instrument of fear.

The mind is always seeking and developing various forms of security, with their values and illusions; the security of wealth with its personal advantages and power; the security of knowledge; the security of belief and ideals; and the security that the mind seeks in love. The mind, which is the instrument and fruit of desire and fear, is repeatedly trying to make itself secure through belief, hope, illusion, knowledge, ideals, patterns, which are the cloaks with which we hope to hide our fears.

The mind, seeking certainty through property, work, through

people, through ideas, does not want to be disturbed and made uncertain. Have you noticed how the mind rebels against anything new—a new idea, a new experience, a new state? When it does experience a new state, the mind immediately brings it into the field of what it knows. The mind is always functioning in the field of security, the known, which is its own projections. It can never experience something beyond itself. You seek certainty because in that state the mind need never be disturbed; you don't face anxiety; you cover up fear; so you never experience the new.

Through the desire to be satisfied, the mind develops its own technique, its own mechanism of resistance and nonresistance, which is the will. Psychological mind is essentially an instrument of fear. Desire produces the psychological mind and in turn psychological mind produces desire. Each engenders the other, creating and continuing the process of the search for self-satisfaction.

Psychological mind seeks a conclusion, a finality on which it can rest, and with that motive it acts. It creates a system of beliefs and these beliefs color all its activities. Mind demands values so that it will not be at a loss, so that it will always have a guide to follow, to imitate. Values are molds in which the mind stagnates.

When the psychological mind imparts values, it can only impart them through the form of memory, and therefore cannot understand the full significance of environment, which is constantly changing. Each mind creates a new set of values— according to its own reaction to environment, and from these created values spring the division of people, class distinctions, fierce antagonisms between creeds, doctrines, nations. Your mind in its lack of perception, in its laziness, desires to conform and keep old patterns, old molds of thought. To each experience you bring that which you are, a conditioned memory, and with this memory you respond and interpret all experiences.

This psychological memory, which you call mind, is constantly giving and imparting values and opinions. That is the function of memory. Mind, instead of being itself intelligence, which is direct perception, is clouded by psychological memory. It gives values as true and false, essential and unessential, according to its calculations, fears, and its search for security. What you call mind is the function of psychological memory but is not real mind at all.

If you examine it, you will see that psychological mind is constantly accepting or rejecting authority and environment. It is constantly conditioning itself by new values and standards born of craving for its self-protection.

When you are evading struggle, conflict, sorrow and when you are seeking comfort, you create various avenues of escape. These avenues of escape become your illusions. Through religion, with its beliefs and ideals, you have found authorized escape from the incessant battle of the present. Through possessive love, ego exaltation is developed and maintained to cover over your poverty of being, to escape emptiness and inner loneliness. Through acquisitiveness and possession of things you hope to escape from the uncertainties of life. This is the psychological mechanism of escape upon which you base your life.

The psychological mind is that limited consciousness that we call the "I." It creates false values, false ideals, self-protective illusions, all to which mind becomes a slave. It has created this almost ceaseless battle of desires and denials, hopes and frustrations, regimentation, disciplines. A disciplined mind (not a mind that is disciplined to carry out a technique—a technique to become a doctor, lawyer, scientist, teacher, etc.) is a mind that has been trained along a particular pattern, and that pattern is the outcome of a false society, false ideas, false concepts. Within that limited pattern, the psychological mind is seeking satisfaction.

The psychological mind seeks satisfaction at any cost, and if thwarted in one direction, it seeks it in another. The whole effort, all the directive power of the mind, is to be satisfied. So satisfaction becomes a mechanical habit of the mind. And when the mind discovers that in the process of satisfaction there is suffering, then it begins to develop an opposite "detachment." Thus there is the positive and negative will ever exerting, ever seeking satisfaction. Will and fear go together. Will and effort are the mechanisms of the mind seeking satisfaction and attempting to get rid of fear.

But psychological mind cannot get rid of fear, for any attempt to destroy fear would necessitate the destruction of the mind itself, which cannot be done. In its attempt to destroy fear, it cultivates the opposites, which are part of fear itself; thus the mind divides itself, creates within itself the dual process. Through constant self-protective action the mind has divided itself into separate thought and separate emotion.

Psychological mind, through its own desires, has broken itself up into different parts, i.e., acceptance and denial, desire and desirelessness, dominance and submission, etc. Because psychological mind has created innumerable escapes, it has created the idea that thought and a thinker are apart from emotion, feeling; that thought is apart from action, and hence our life is broken up, incomplete.

Psychological mind has divided itself into three divisions. First, creating ideals, purposes, culminations, attainments, ends, which is the pursuit of objectives. Second, the creation of turmoil, conflict, disturbance, disharmony, which is the outcome of fear, frustration, suffering. Third, the creation of me, myself, self-consciousness, which is the "I" process.

This whole dilemma in which mind is caught is the result of ignorance. A conditioned mind cannot experience completely. Any effort to put away satisfaction is only another way of being satisfied, giving strength to the conditioned mind. Therefore, any problems that the psychological mind tackles can only increase those problems. As long as the psychological mind deals with any problem, at any level, it can only create more trouble, more misery and more confusion. We must understand that whatever the psychological mind does to control its own thought, can only make it more narrow, limited, conditioned.

There are three attitudes of the mind: "I know," "I believe," "I do not know." When you say, "I know," you mean you know through experience, and through that experience you become certain and convinced of an idea, a belief. Your experience may be based on imagination, wish fulfillment, which to you gradually becomes "fact." When you say, "I believe," your action is based on hidden hopes and craving for continuity, certainty. But if you say, "I do not know," fully comprehending its significance, then there is a possibility of perceiving what it is. To be in a state of not knowing demands great denudation and continuous awareness. This "not knowing" is not a negative state; it is a most vital and earnest state. Then the mind-heart is open and does not grasp at opinions, explanations and assertions.

The mind, which is intelligent, does not seek security. It reveals to itself its own fears and wants. Out of this arises integral awareness of its impermanency. This recognition alone can set the mind free from its self-created bondage.

To understand the complexity of life, the mind must be

extremely pliable and simple. Simplicity of mind is not the emptiness of negation, renunciation, nor is it acceptance. It is the fullness of comprehension. It is intelligence. To an intelligent mind, environment yields its significance. Such a mind is free of environment, is not conditioned by environment. In this pliability and simplicity is true adjustment, not the adjustment to a particular pattern or condition, but the adjustment through understanding what really is, which is therefore free of any particular condition.

Psychological mind is essentially desire, intention, inclination and purpose. It is sentiment, disposition, like and dislike, want and not want, thought and feeling. Psychological mind is the intellect with all its faculties and comparative process of thinking. It is the intellectual function, which enables the mind to receive, revive or modify perceptions, conceptions, opinions and conclusions. Mind is all states, relations and functions of psychological consciousness. When the mind is utterly free of the many hindrances and limitations, when it has lost all support, explanations, when it is open, wholly naked, when it is vulnerable by understanding the cause of self-created illusions, only then is there reality.

The conscious mind, influenced by the subconscious, creates the faculty that we call the intellect, the capacity to think. The intellect is the faculty that receives sensory impressions and conceives and reviews; that is, it is the faculty that forms, associates, remembers, correlates, compares, interprets and comprehends ideas. It is the faculty that modifies, changes, shapes, subjugates, determines, controls. It reasons, analyzes, judges, chooses, makes effort, discriminates, justifies and rationalizes. It is the faculty that reflects, introspects, concentrates, imagines and fantasizes. It is the faculty that creates the duality process and functions through it as the comparative process of thinking, the process of the conflict of opposites.

Analysis is the very negation of complete action. There is no understanding in the analysis of a past experience, it is dead. Therefore self-analysis is destructive. If you analyze action you will never act; your action will become slowly restricted and will finally result in the death of action. The same thing applies to your mind, your thought, your emotion. When you begin to analyze you put an end to movement; when you try to analyze an intense feeling, that feeling dies.

In your attempt to achieve a balance between thought and feeling, you think you must analyze. But analysis always limits action. Do not try to analyze your action. Rather, if you want to find out whether you are class-conscious, whether you are self-righteous, whether you are nationalistic, bigoted, authority bound, imitative—if you are really interested in discovering these hindrances, then become fully aware, become conscious at the time of what you are doing. Don't be merely observant, don't merely look at your action objectively from the outside, but become fully aware, both mentally and emotionally, aware with your whole being in the moment of action. In this awareness you will see that many memories are involved, many conditioning factors, which prevent you from acting fully, completely.

Self-analysis and awareness are two different things; the one is morbid, the other is joyous, releasing. Self-analysis takes place before or after action; out of that analysis, mind creates a pattern to which a future action is forced to conform, thus there comes about a rigidity of thought and action. Self-analysis is always deadening. It only leads to the creation of patterns and imitation, and so there is no release from bondage, frustration. Self-analysis or introspection takes place before or after action, thus preparing the future or limiting it.

Introspection is a self-analysis in which thought is measuring its own action and its results, according to pleasure and pain, reward and punishment, thus forming a judgment, a pattern. Having examined the action of the past, thought tries to carry out, through present action, what it has learned, and so determines how it shall act in the future. You are always analyzing a past or future action; you cannot analyze an action that is being lived.

Imaginative action is another escape from the problems of life. Imagination can become creative and effective, only when it has liberated itself from fears and illusions, which tradition and self-protective desire have imposed upon it.

That which is generally considered intuition is the fulfillment of your own secret hopes and desires. Intuition, as commonly understood, is based on the past, the past accumulation of experiences. It is a warning to act carefully in the present. Intuition may also only be a self-deceiving wish.

Most people separate intuition from intelligence. They feel that intuition gives them a certain security and hope. Many people act "on intuition," a "hunch." That is, they act without depth of thought. Many people accept a theory, or a thought, because they say their "intuition tells them that it is true." There is no reason behind it. They accept a theory or idea because it gives them some solution, some comfort. It is not reason that is functioning, but it is their own hope, their own longing that is directing their mind.

There is creative intuition, but only if all desire and craving have ceased. Then intuition is intelligence. Intelligence does not arise from past experience, it is the understanding of past experience. If you base your action on the past, on what you call intuition, it is bound to lead you astray. Whereas if there is spontaneous action in the ever-moving present, in that action there is intelligence and that intelligence is intuition. This intelligence is not to be separated from intuition.

The retiring into privacy to contemplate upon some ideal, some object, some idea, is an escape. The man who withdraws from the daily contact with life makes his life unnatural. Real contemplation is the very essence of action. Contemplation comes out of meeting life fully. Contemplation is action.

Concentration is the focusing of all energies on something in which you are interested. When your interest is in making money, or when you are absorbed in a book or in some achievement, there is natural concentration. You make an effort to attend to the objective. But in creative activity, one is the action, and concentration is the natural fulfillment. Such concentration is the fulfillment of action, not the fulfillment of purposeful achievement.

CHAPTER 9

Thought Process

*Man's psychological use of the "I," the thinker identity, is
as old as his awakening of consciousness, and it has become
the destructive center to which he now clings. From this
primitive beginning to the present, man has continued and
elaborated this center, the "I," and has become this thinking-
feeling process of self-centered interest.*

Long ago, as the result of innate formative processes operating in man, his consciousness reached a stage of development in which he woke up to both the outer and inner environmental forces. He began to be cognizant of his inner experiences and of the outer world. He became conscious of various sensations and the stimuli that produced these sensations. Conscious differentiation and ideation began to take place. His interpretations of these sensations and their stimuli, which at best were vague impressions and ideas, were the beginnings of consciousness, intellectual thought.

Prior to conscious awakening, man's response to stimuli was of an unconscious, automatic nature, purely reflexive instinctual responses. But as he awakened, he correlated these sensations with their stimuli and began to form crude ideas about them. Through rudimentary ideation, through initial conscious perception, thoughts were formed. This led to correlation and association of perceptions, which in turn formed concepts, ideas. That is, man began consciously to interpret, name and give significance to that which he was experiencing. His thoughts, his ideas, reflected the significance of his impressions. The nature of these interpretations was the psychological sensory counterpart of the stimuli that produced them. That is, sensation became the media through which thought was formed. It became awakened consciousness. Thus thought became the reciprocal sensory counterpart to awakened sensation. For thought is not something vastly different and apart from sensation. It is the product of sensation, created out of the nature of sensation. Thoughts, ideas, are the extensions of sensations, sensations of different kinds and qualities. Functionally, thought verifies its sensory source. Both thought and the physical senses act reciprocally upon each other and both respond to each other. Sensation produces thought and thought produces sensation. Like begets like. This is a fundamental law of substance, of nature. Thought is substance, sensory substance. Thought is another form of sensation.

With the awakening of consciousness, man only became awakened to that which already existed. But to him it was entirely new. Actually the only change that had taken place was a change of consciousness in which there was initial understanding of what was taking place about him and within him. That is, he awakened and became aware of his unconscious, instinctive reflex patterns, their processes and significances. Having no other means with which to meet life and make determinations, no other media with which to interpret the significances of experiences, his criteria of understanding, his thoughts and thinking processes just being formed, were of necessity intrinsically the same in nature and action as the former unconscious living processes. Actually he had only awakened to his former unconscious living processes. He patterned his thoughts and ideas upon and through his perceptions of them. Hence consciousness became the expanded and mirrored reflection in thought of the inner instinctive state and processes, and the impressions of outer environment. That is why even today man lives more instinctively, more animal like, than human. He has only the thin covering of supposedly cultured behavior to guide him. He is more unconscious than conscious of what he is doing.

If you observe an unconscious reflex pattern properly, you will recognize it as being unconscious memory in action. The action fulfilled by its function is but the constant imitative repetition of the same action operating through its own volition, which has been established as a habit process. Hence in the unconscious reflex pattern, we see that it contains memory, imitation, repetition and habit—the very same psychological processes evident in our psychological, intellectual processes of thinking. This holds true of all other basic functional capacities. If we extend this observation to all organic life, we will recognize a capacity inherent in all things to retain the essential elements of need from experience, and to fulfill them repeatedly essentially in the same manner. It is inherent memory in action and the capacity to do the same thing over and over again. Hence memory, factual memory, habit and the imitative process have existed in all manifestation from the beginning. The thought process, as we know it, came much later.

It is also necessary to recognize in the fulfillment of organic and physiological law that innumerable other processes had to operate simultaneously and cooperatively in order that the unconscious organism could maintain its integrity. The instinctive capacity to differentiate, to discriminate, to judge, to interpret, etc., and the ability to act in accordance with the need in these determinations, was also necessary. All these capacities are in the unconscious organism and existed in man prior to his awakening. He has but continued their use, both physiologically and psychologically. If we look at man's psychological processes of behavior and thinking, his psychological self-protective processes of today, we find exactly the same processes operating as were used by him in his unconscious, instinctive state. Man's intellectual processes are not greatly different from those of his former unconscious state and activities. The difference is only the manner in which they are applied. Man's consciousness is but an imitative process of instinctual expression, in which self-protection and self-perpetuation are the primary motivations, except for one glaring exception: essential need has been converted into all-consuming psychological desire. Man's intellectual processes, when considered in their basic drives, are essentially just as elemental in their components and fulfillment; they are only an extension of his instinctual nature. These components have now been totally converted into the fulfillment of psychological satisfactions. Even though man considers himself enlightened, he is not removed from ignorance for he spends most of his time in competition, rivalry, war. He believes that this is the natural thing to do. He knows very little about himself, and practically nothing about how to live with his fellow man. His awakening is more physiological and environmental, than intelligent and enlightened.

In the beginning, man's awakened consciousness did not have the capacity to understand that his thoughts and ideas were only correlated counterparts of the sensations he was experiencing. Nor did he recognize and understand that whatever was taking place in his consciousness, be it thought, action or the thing observed, he was that which he was experiencing. Even the man of today does not recognize this fact.

Early in life man began to recognize that he had experiences different from another. It was then that he began to differentiate himself from all others, and from all things. He recognized that he was one of a similar kind, but also that he was different in many ways from his fellow men. All his experiences gave emphasis to these differences. So as man became conscious of his being, it was natural for him to separate himself from all things, from all others of the human species and to establish an identity. He considered himself to be an observer, an experiencer, an individual in his own right. He regarded himself as a thinker who used thought as an instrument of the thinker. It was then that separation of the thinker and his thought took place. Through this difference of identity, the establishment of individuality took place. It was then that the "I" process was born in the thinker and his qualities, pride, self-importance, vanity, greed and all the rest of the "I" process. Man's psychological use of the "I," the thinker identity, is as old as his awakening of consciousness, and it has become the destructive center to which he now clings.

From this primitive beginning to the present, man has continued and elaborated this center, the "I," and has become this thinking-feeling process of self-centered interest. From this early beginning he has established himself as the thinker, the interpreter. And it is this erroneous psychological process and attitude of mind that prevents him from realizing that he has established a self-centered barrier to the understanding and the solution of his problems.

This primary obstructive psychological factor or device consists of man setting himself apart from his thoughts, the creation and maintenance of a "thinker apart from his thoughts." Man lives and acts as if he, the thinker, and his thoughts are separate, not one and the same thing. Hence man believes that through the use of thought he can solve the problems of relationship. He thinks that by manipulating, molding, adjusting, changing thought, he will be able to find the solution to all his problems. He considers himself as having a distinctive ability and identity; the Thinker, the Reasoner. As such he sets out to shape life, according to his desire, his will; to make life what he wants it to be, which primarily is the fulfillment of his self-centered interests. He fails to see that all men are doing the same thing, fulfilling their greedy interests. He does not see that nothing can come from this but constant conflict, chaos and suffering. In spite of the overwhelming evidence of the faultiness of this form of thinking, man continues in it and carries on, regardless of the fact that for all his efforts and every conceivable type of ideology, he has not solved in depth a single psychological problem of relationship.

Through this self-centered psychological process of the thinker being separate from his thoughts, man has been able to create a thinking process that meets the needs of his self-centered desires. Through this process he can avoid or ameliorate the consequences of his thoughts, feelings and actions. Separating himself from his thinking he can alter, transform, rationalize and justify anything he has done or wants to do. His present process of the thinker being independent from his thoughts is an escape from responsibility for his actions. It is a trick of the mind, which not only avoids the responsibility of his acts, but at the same time it enables him to continue his constant search for security, for power, domination, for the possession of things and the control of people, whatever the means necessary to achieve these, no matter the suffering and conflict it creates. The thinker apart from his thought blinds him to what he is doing, how he is doing it and why he does it. It keeps him in a constant state of frustration and conflict.

CHAPTER 10

New Approach

*What is the new approach, which will lead us to the central
problem? The barrier to a new approach is our conditioned
thinking. What you and I are is the outcome of many yesterdays.
We are the total summation of the past. We do not meet
life without conditioning, conditioning being knowledge,
experience, belief, tradition, identification with a particular
party, group or nation, race, ideology, and so on. We meet life
with a particular background and training, with experiences.
We have such an accumulation of knowledge, so many
prejudices, so many ideologies, so many beliefs to which we cling.*

Most of us are confronted with many problems, not only individual, but collective; there are problems that not only touch our personal lives, but also affect us as citizens of a particular country, as part of a collective group. We have problems that are sociological and economic, and spiritual. We are confronted with problems of every kind; and the more we deal with them, the more they seem to increase and multiply and become more confused. Man's economic, political, social and religious affairs are in a constant state of turmoil, confusion, adjustment and failure. His life is one of uncertainty, frustration, division, conflict and destruction.

Because the individual has not solved his problem, the world problem has not been solved. The individual problem *is* the world problem. You cannot separate the individual from the world. The individual and the world are one. In the solution of the individual problem, the world problem will be solved. And the individual problem can be solved, and so can the problem of the world.

Each one of us is conscious of a particular difficulty, and wants to grapple with that difficulty on its own, as something separate. Actually, there is only one fundamental problem, which expresses itself in many ways. What is needed is a totally new approach, in which this central problem can be solved.

Our difficulty lies in not thinking of these problems anew, in not thinking of ourselves from a different point of view.

What is the new approach, which will lead us to the central problem? The barrier to a new approach is our conditioned thinking. What you and I are is the outcome of many yesterdays. We are the total summation of the past. We do not meet life without conditioning, conditioning being knowledge, experience, belief, tradition, identification with a particular party, group or nation, race, ideology, and so on. We meet life with a particular background and training, with particular experiences. We have such an accumulation of knowledge, so many prejudices, so many ideologies, so many beliefs to which we cling.

These backgrounds, this conditioning, prevents us from meeting and seeing life as it actually is. The society about us is the outcome of our desires to be secure, to be safe, to be permanent in our particular form of conditioning. Most of us are unaware that we are conditioned, and that our conditioning is the result of our own desires, of our own longings to be secure, safe. We never look at life except through our particular conditioning. Hence problems, whether social, religious, moral or economic, whether individual or collective, are judged by what we are. They are not going to be solved by isolated consideration or by depending on a particular system. This is one of the fundamental errors of our thinking. They must be solved as a whole, as related to all other problems. One must deeply comprehend one's own process of creating the problem and being caught up with it. It is here that we have been mistaken, for we cannot solve any problem completely on its own level, contending only with the particular factors of the problem, apart from the maker of the problem, ourselves.

What we must realize is that to understand any problem, we have to understand the cause. The problem is not different from the maker of the problem. Problems are not created by themselves. They are an effect, a result, which have a cause, and each problem will be consistent with the cause, the maker of the problem. When we understand the creator of the problem, then we will understand the problem; then we will be able to resolve the problem. There cannot be a problem unless its cause, ourselves, is understood. The problem arises out of us. We are the problem.

To find the solution for any problem, individual or collective, we must understand ourselves, which in all cases is the real cause of the problem.

You must first understand the process of your thinking, the activity of you, the thinker, and your thought. That is the obvious approach. We must understand that the kind of effort we are now making is erroneous. The right approach is not my approach, it is not your approach, it is the only relevant approach, and intelligence is not yours or mine. The study of yourself is far more significant than the study of any particular problem, or the study of all problems.

The thinker is always separating himself as the "me," the "I," and remaining outside the action. The thinker thinks himself an entity, separate from thought—that he is an observer of thought, that he is the experiencer outside the experience.

As long as there is a thinker as the "I," the "me," there is a center from which action is always taking place. That center is the result of your thinking, and our thinking is the outcome of our conditioning.

As long as there is a thinker, a center, apart from thought, a thinker examining thought, then whatever the outcome of the examination may be, it is inevitably conditioned and therefore inadequate. As long as you establish a thinker independent of his thoughts, you are bound to have conflict between the thinker and his thought.

The moment you separate the thinker from thought you have the whole problem of trying to control, dissipate, suppress thought, or of trying to be free from a particular thought. This separation inevitably creates the problem of choice and where there is choice there must be conflict. Choice will never lead to understanding because choice implies a thinker who chooses. As long as the thinker separates himself from his thoughts, so long will the vain conflict of the opposites continue. Our life is a conflict, a series of battles between the thinker and his thought—what to do and what not to do, what should be, and what should not be. This is the conflict between the thinker and his thought in which we are caught—it is our whole problem.

But to face your problems you must be unconditionally free. If in any way you have fear, you cannot solve any of your problems. To be integrated in your whole being is to be unconditioned. If in any way, in any manner, you have doubt, craving, fear, these create a conditioned mind, which prevents the ultimate solution of any problem.

The solution of all problems and the liberation from them can be found only in the release from the maker of the problem, the center of doubt, craving, fear. What is important is not to solve any particular problem, but to deal with the primary problem, the maker of the problem. Before we try to understand any problem, the problem of war, the economic problem, the religious problem, the social problem, the problems of love, duty, marriage and so on, we must first understand the thinker, the maker, the analyzer of the problem. The important thing is not to seek a solution to the problem, but to understand the maker of the problem. It is this contradiction that must be understood—the thinker using thought.

Most of us try to solve a problem superficially, with the conscious mind, with the intellect, "the thinker."

Through relationship you get to know the maker of the problem because the maker of the problem exists only in relationship. It is only in relationship that problems arise. It is only then that the maker, the cause, can be discerned creating and continuing the problems. Hence understanding relationship is the beginning of self-knowledge, the beginning of the new approach. Relationship is a mirror for self-revealment, self-exposure, and not exposure of the other.

When you see certain distortions in yourself, which you don't like, you want to be free of them. You try to analyze or to discipline them, to do something about the distortions. To be free of a particular distortion, you must first discover for yourself the truth that the thinker is not separate from thought; then you will see that what you call a distortion is a process of thinking, and that there is no thinker apart from that process of thinking.

So, the real problem is to understand and dissolve that center, which is the thinker, the maker of all problems. And the first consideration, the first question is, what is thought and what is the thinker? Is the thinker separate from thought, or is he the outcome of thinking?

We have to find out whether thought produces the thinker or whether the thinker, being separate, apart, is independent of thought, and therefore can control it. Is the thinker the outcome of thought, or is he an entity in his own right, not created by thought, but outside all thought?

You think that the thinker is separate from thought; therefore you control thought, you shape thought, you subjugate thought, push thought aside. The thinker, you say, is different from thought. But is that so?

Before we discuss further, we will have to find out if the "me," the examiner, the observer, the analyzer, the thinker, is different from thought qualities. Is the thinker, the experiencer, different from thought, from experience, from the thing observed? Is the "me"—whether you place it at the highest or the lowest level—different from the qualities that compose it?

Mind, seeing itself as transient, divides itself and creates the thinker as a permanent entity, and gives to the thinker continuity as the "I." Thought has created the thinker as a separate entity because thought is always changing, modifying. You see your own impermanence and so create the thinker as an entity to which you give permanency. So you, the thinker, become an entity apart from your thought. Then you, the thinker, the supposed separate entity, act on thought, choosing this particular thought and rejecting that, proceed to control, modify and dominate thought. You maintain the mind in a constant state of agitation, constant search, inquiry, longing, wanting. We have created the thinker, which is only a belief. Mind, seeking security, holds to this belief that there is a thinker separate from thought. This is one of the cunning tricks of the mind so that the thinker can change his garb according to circumstances, stances, yet remain the same. Outwardly there is the appearance of change but inwardly the thinker continues to be as he is.

Actually there is no thinker apart from experience, apart from thought—there is only the experience of thought, thinking. For is there a thinker without thought? If you have no thought, where is the thinker? So the thinker does not create thought—thought creates the thinker. So the thinker is thought, the experiencer *is* the experienced, the observer *is* the observed, the analyzer *is* the analyzed, they are not two separate processes, but a single unitary process. For example, as long as there is an analyzer, a thinker, examining the past, surely the analyzer, thinker, is also the result of the past; therefore whatever he analyzes, thinks about, examines, must be conditioned, and seen in terms of conditioning, thought about in terms of ideas resulting from the past. The thinker and thought are similar in content and function, and so are one.

As of now we have observed the thinker operating upon thought; and this we see creates conflicts between the thinker and thought, keeping the mind in a constant state of frustration. The thinker, the "I," is arbitrary, artificial and entirely fictitious. We also see that the thinker is the product of thought. There is no thinker if there is no thought, no experiencer if there is no experiencing. So if we see the truth of this, that the thinker is the thought that there is no thinker separate from thought, but only the process of thinking, then what happens?

Is not the process of conflict removed? When we see there is only thinking, have we not removed the cause of conflict? When we are aware of the full significance of this contradiction in ourselves, that there is no thinker, only thinking, does it not bring an extraordinary change? You are yourself then—not something you are trying to be, not the thinker manipulating thought. When you remove that entity that creates conflict, surely then, there is the possibility of understanding and freeing yourself from this basic contradiction.

If you can see and understand the truth that the thinker is the thought, the analyzer *is* the analyzed—if you can understand that, not merely verbally through reading or discussing, but in actual experience, then you will discover that an extraordinary revolution is taking place, that there is only thinking, and not a thinker.

The moment you see there is no thinker separate from thought, that there is only thinking—then all choice is removed. There is only thinking and not the translation of thought—then there is no entity that says "I" will choose this thought and reject others. There is no translator, no interpreter, no judge, no bearer of the club. Then you will see there is no conflict between the thinker and the thought, and therefore the mind is no longer trying to change, trying to become, justifying, no longer caught in the world of manipulation. Then there is only thinking. Then you will see, if this transformation takes place, that there is no longer an effort, but an extraordinary alert passivity. Then you are able to be consciously aware of thought and not as the thinker observing thought from the outside. There is then understanding of every relationship, of every incident that arises. Therefore the mind is always fresh to meet things new. The thought process does not come into being when there is recognition of "what is." If I accept what I am, then thought is not; but something else takes place when I accept "what is." Then the thinker and his thought are inseparable, the thinker has become his thought, then duality has been transcended. The basic contradiction has been resolved.

This is the fundamental revolution, which is essential in order to understand the whole process of thinking. The cessation of the thinker means there is only thought. Then there will be the removal of unconscious conditioned resistance to self-exposure, self-revealment; then the mind will let go; then there is no thinker trying to dissect, to analyze or shape a particular thought; then there will be no thinker trying to protect and continue himself, trying to be secure. Fear, doubt and craving will have been removed. Then it is possible for one to be aware, and therefore it is possible for psychological thought to come to an end, without the process of struggle, without the process of analysis. Then there is only thinking.

The ending of psychological thought is not a process of living in an ivory tower of abstraction; on the contrary, the ending of thought is the highest form of understanding, which can only be fulfilled in the action of relationship. And with the ending of thought there can be creativeness. Therefore the understanding of thought and how to bring it to an end is important, for only when the thinker, that continuity as an entity, as "I" in thought, comes to an end is there creativeness. And as long as psychological thought is functioning there can be no creativeness. Thought is the result of continuity, all of our memory and past conditioning. Creativeness is a state of mind in which thought is absent.

So when we understand the mind, not as the thinker, but only as thought, when there is no thinker observing, judging, molding thought, but only choiceless awareness of the mind, without any sense of condemnation or justification, without any choice, then the thought process as we know it comes to an end. Mind then is without contradiction. Quietness of mind is not a thing to be cultivated but comes into being naturally when you understand fundamentally that the thinker is his thought, and that the "I" is self-fabricated. Thought, thinking, as a reaction to a particular conditioning comes to an end, creativeness is present and the problem is understood.

We all have problems, which are never completely solved. Because we, as individuals, have not solved our own problems, the world problems have not been solved. What is needed is a new approach—we must think of these problems anew, thinking of ourselves from a different point of view. We must think of our problems integrally, from the whole, if there is to be a solution. This presents considerable difficulty because of our conditioned thinking. But if we are to understand the problems, we will have to understand the cause, the maker of the problems—ourselves— for we are the maker of the problems. We have to understand our thinking, the activity of the thinker, the "I," and his thought. We find the thinker separates himself from thought, cannot solve the problems and keeps the mind in turmoil. Hence we see the solution of all problems is in our release from the thinker, the "I," the maker of the problems. We find the thinker is the product of thought, that he is arbitrary, artificial and entirely fictitious, for there is only thinking. With the thinker gone, the process of conflict is removed, the protective conditioned response is gone. What is left is you, not something you are trying to be. This removes the contradiction, then there is only "what is." In this transformation there is alert passivity, choiceless awareness, in which there is understanding. If you accept what you are, then duality is transcended, thought as we know it has come to an end and creativeness is present.

We should understand our process of thinking, and perhaps be able to go beyond it. What is this thing that we worship, this intellect to which we look up? What is this psychological thought, this thinking that has created our problems and which now tries to solve them? Until we understand that, we cannot find another way of living, another way to exist. Seeing that thought has not freed man, you and me, from our conflicts, we must understand the whole process of our thinking.

We have whole systems of psychological thought cultivated through the ages, to which each one of us has contributed. In this ruthless movement each one, consciously or unconsciously, is caught up. There is an individual and a collective consciousness sometimes running parallel, often diametrically opposed.

What is the basis, the root of your psychological thought process? It is important to discover this. If the root of the tree is diseased or decayed, of what value is it to trim its branches? Likewise, should you not first discern the origin of your thinking before concerning yourself with its various expressions and alterations? In understanding truly the source, through deep awareness, your human thought will become free of illusion and fear. Each one has to discover this source for himself and transform radically the process of thinking.

Desire is sensation, and sensation is the basis of thought, of the mind. Sensation is the foundation of all your thinking. Psychological thought springs from the sensation of want and not want, from the sensation of what is me and mine, and what is not me and not mine. Thought itself is response to sensation. Thought and sensation are one—only thought is the qualification of sensation. Thought gives qualities to sensation. So thought is qualified sensation. Thought and its processes is the extension of psycho-emotional sensations, reactions, in consciousness. Thought is sensation. Thought is psychological desire in reaction.

The basis of our thinking is craving, which creates the self. The "I," the thinker, thought expresses itself through worldliness, in possessive love and in the belief in continuity. Thought is deeply and actively concerned with the idea of continuity of itself in different forms, gross and subtle. Is not this your main preoccupation is life, the continuity of the self in possessions, in relationship, in ideas? You crave for certainty.

Thought in your daily life is occupied with the creation of tradition, the continuance, and the modification of tradition. Thought moves from certainty to certainty, from the known to the known, from one substitution to another, and thus is never still; it is ever pursuing, ever wandering. This chattering of the mind destroys creative intelligence.

What happens to thought, to the mind occupied with itself and its expressions, conscious or unconscious? It gives great value and importance to itself. Thought, thus occupied, must engender confusion, conflict, sorrow. Being caught in its own net, it tries to escape into the future or into those activities that assure immediate forgetfulness, so-called social service, worship of state or person, racial and social antagonism, and so on. Thus psychological thought gets more and more entangled in its own desires and escapes. As long as thought is preoccupied with its own personal importance and continuity, it is incapable of becoming aware of its own process.

Observe your own thought. You will see that it springs from fear, from craving, affection, hope, from like and dislike, from the sensation of what is mine and not mine. This independent thought divides itself endlessly into the high and low, the good and bad, the right and wrong, the superior and inferior, conscious and unconscious, and so there is conflict.

The conscious influenced by the subconscious creates the intellect, the faculty to discern, to discriminate, to choose, to judge, to interpret, to rationalize, to justify. The intellect is the very instrument of conflict.

You have separated your thought from your feeling, thus setting up another entity, separate from your action. You divide your life into three distinct parts, thinking, feeling and acting. The three are one: to think, to feel, to act—there is no distinction. There is action when you are thinking—there is action when you are feeling. Therefore you may be working, moving, acting, or you may be alone and quiet; and these states can be action. When you understand this you will not make a separation between thinking, acting and feeling.

Thought as a process is a process of reaction. There is a challenge, a stimulus, and a response. The response is the process of thinking. If there is no stimulus, no challenge of any kind, conscious or unconscious, violent or very subtle, there is no response, that is, there is no thinking. So thinking is a response to a challenge. Thinking, thought, is a process of reaction to any form of stimulus or challenge.

Conditioned thought creates the process of psychological time. It is the response of the background, ideas, beliefs. This response of the background is the process of psychological time. Thinking is the use of this background, the past. Hence the thinker, the self, only exists as this background and as the process of psychological time.

As such thought is the self, thought is the word that identifies itself as the "me," the "I." No matter at whatever level the self is placed, high or low, it is still within the field of psychological thought. Self, thought, is very complex; it is not of any one level, but is made up of many thoughts, many entities, each in contradiction with the other. The self, the "me," the "I," is made up of the qualities, tendencies, prejudices, idiosyncrasies, ideas, beliefs, the whole background of the mind.

Functionally, psychological human thought is in constant movement; it is never still; it is always searching, longing for security, certainty. So for you every thought has some significance, some value, some hidden meaning.

Now if you can understand each thought, each experience, and not resist it, not push it away; if you can look at each experience as it is, as it arises and uncover its meaning, then you will see that those thoughts, those experiences, never come back—they are finished. Only thoughts not understood come back.

Psychological human thought can only discover its own projections. It cannot discover anything new. Thought recognizes that which it has experienced, it cannot recognize that which it has not experienced. Psychological thought is time, its projections are time. Therefore it cannot go beyond itself. Thought can only recognize that which it has created—psychological time.

Your psychological thought, desire thought, cannot possibly understand reality. Do what you will, it cannot go beyond itself. It can only create reality in its own image but it will not be reality. It will be only self-projection.

Real thought can understand its own process only if it does not identify itself with, and cling to, any of its own creations, any of its desires. Real thought, not psychological thought, does not belong to any nation or to any race; it does not follow any particular groove or established ideas, habits, traditions. Real thought is critical; it is a thing apart from inherited or acquired knowledge. Real thought is not reaction but action. Action is real thought. Psychological thought is reaction, desire, not action. Does not action imply thought? Is not action thought itself? You cannot act without thought, thinking. I know most people do, but theirs is reaction, it is not intelligent, nor harmonious; it is psychological static. Thought is action, which is constant movement.

When there is real thought, action, not psychological thought, not reaction, there will be creative thinking. Creative thinking is the infinite movement of thought, emotion and action. When thought, which is emotion, which is action itself, is unimpeded in its movement, when it is not compelled or influenced or bound by an idea, and does not proceed from the background of tradition or habit, then that movement is creative. So long as thought is circumscribed, held by a fixed idea, or merely adjusts itself to a background or condition, such thought is not creative.

The movement of creative thinking does not seek in its expression a result, an achievement; its results and expressions are not its culmination. It has no culmination or goal, for it is always in movement.

Again, creative thinking is free of division, which creates conflict between thought, emotion and action. Division exists only when there is the search for a goal, when there is adjustment and the complacency of security.

When this movement of thought is clear, simple, direct, spontaneous, profound, then there is no conflict in the individual or in his relationships, for action then is the very expression of this living, creative movement.

There is no "art" of thinking, there is only creative thinking. There is no technique of thinking, but only spontaneous creative functioning intelligence, which is the harmony of reason, emotion and action not divided or divorced from each other. And to think creatively is to bring about harmony between mind, emotion and action.

For creative thinking to be, psychological thought must end. And in order that this may be, we must understand thought, its significances, the relationship of the thinker to his thought, and that which comes from it. Psychological thought, the self, the "I," ends only when we understand the whole process of thinking. So through constant awareness, thought must free itself from worldliness and discern greed and need; thought must free itself from possessive love; thought must free itself from the craving for personal immortality through religion, through reincarnation, through property, power, family, race, through the continuation of the "I."

To understand reality, for that immensity to come into being, one must understand the process of one's own thinking.

CHAPTER 11

Suffering

Suffering is a shock to awaken you, to help you to understand life. Whatever gives a great shock, which you call suffering, will keep you awake to meet life fully, if you do not seek an escape from it. It will help you to discard the many illusions that you have created about yourself. It is not only suffering or conflict that keeps you awake. Anything that gives you a shock, should make you question the false standards and values that you have created in your search for security.

The fundamental cause of man's suffering is his egotism, expressing itself in many ways, essentially in his search for security through immortality, possessiveness and by following some form of "ism."

Where there is disturbance or threat to man's security through the action of life, he calls that suffering. He fails, however, to see that suffering is a disturbance, a threat to his sense of security. Suffering is an indication of a stagnant and attached mind, and instead of realizing this, man seeks another form of drug to put the mind to sleep.

When you suffer, as everyone does, you seek an immediate remedy and comfort. When you feel physical pain, you obtain a palliative at the nearest drugstore to lessen your pain. So also, when you experience mental or emotional anguish, you seek consolation. You are constantly seeking a compensation for your pains. Man tries to get rid of suffering by explanation, drugs, drink, religion, amusement, resignation. Yet suffering continues.

Suffering exists because of lack of understanding of its cause. Most of us suffer economically, spiritually, or in our relationship with each other. Psychological suffering is that high, intense thought and emotion that tries to force you to recognize things as they are. For that state of mind, when there is suffering, there is acuteness of thought, there is an intense turmoil. This intense turmoil is really what causes suffering.

Man, in his constant search for comfort, in his efforts to neutralize suffering, denies the true function, the true fulfillment of suffering, which is to awaken intelligence. When man's entire time is spent neutralizing, or trying to be free of psychological frustration resulting from his desires, he denies the real use of suffering when he does not use it for self-exposure through awareness.

Suffering is a shock to awaken you, to help you to understand life. Whatever gives a great shock, which you call suffering, will keep you awake to meet life fully, if you do not seek an escape from it. It will help you to discard the many illusions that you have created about yourself. It is not only suffering or conflict that keeps you awake. Anything that gives you a shock, should make you question the false standards and values that you have created in your search for security.

Suffering is the companion of all, the rich and the poor, the believer and the nonbeliever. In spite of all your beliefs and doctrines, in spite of your temples and gods, suffering, sorrow, is your constant companion. Let us understand this and not think of being rid of it. When you have fully understood suffering, then you will not seek a way to overcome it.

To understand this threat, this disturbance to our security, which you call suffering, you must begin with yourselves, not with the idea of suffering, for that is only the arid emptiness of the intellect. You must begin with the agonies, miseries and conflicts, which seem to have no end. To discern the process of suffering each one must comprehend himself. To understand oneself is one of the most difficult tasks and demands the most strenuous effort and constant alertness. Very few have the desire to understand deeply this process of suffering and sorrow. To discover the cause of suffering, mind must be acute, pliable, choiceless, not dulled by want, nor deflected by theories. If you would bring sorrow to an end, you must understand the process of division in consciousness, how the thinker separates himself from his thought, the process of duality and the conflict of opposites. These create conflict and make the mind a battlefield of many wants.

When work, which should be the true expression of your being, becomes merely mechanical, stupid and useless, then there is frustration. When your emotional life, which should be rich and complete, is thwarted by conflict and fear, then there is frustration. When mind, which should be alert, pliable, limitless, is weighed down by tradition, self-protective memories, ideals, beliefs, then there is frustration.

Blockages occur because conscious mind does not want to respond to the deeper demands which life is presenting, for they may necessitate a different course of action. And different action might bring about trouble and pain. Or the mind is incapable of wider and deeper thought-feeling. This is lack of capacity, which can be corrected only through persistent and constant awareness, through searching, observing, studying.

Let us not look at disease from the point of view of invoking aid. First of all, if you are normal, then there is a normal miracle taking place in the world; that is, if you are free of all psychological problems, then you travel alone; but you are so abnormal that you want abnormal actions to take place. You suffer psychologically and you are cured, it may be by a doctor, it may be by a psychologist. But if you do not know the psychological cause of your suffering, you will again become ill. You must discover for yourself the cause of psychological suffering; no doctor is ever going to show you the cause of psychological suffering. You may be healed symptomatically for the moment, but unless you find out for yourself what causes your suffering, you will be ill again. In discovering the cause you will become healthy.

You will discover the significance of death by understanding the unhappiness and agony caused by death. When there is death, there is an intense shock, which is called suffering. You have lost someone whom you love greatly, on whom you have relied, who enriched you. When there is suffering, the indication of poverty of being, you seek a remedy. It may be the remedy that religions offer, the final unity of all human beings, with many theories concerning it. Or it may be the spiritualistic drug, and the comfortable remedy in the idea of reincarnation. You seek innumerable escapes from the agony caused by the death of someone whom you love greatly. These escapes are but subtle ways to lose and forget yourself. Your concern is not with the dead, but with your own suffering, which you call love of the dead.

Now if you do not seek consolation, however subtle it may be, then that suffering will awaken your true intelligence, which alone will reveal the flow of reality. Through bereavement you become conscious of your own emptiness, void, loneliness and this causes pain. To be free of this agony, you seek remedies, consolations. You are merely seeking opiates to drug your mind, so the mind becomes a slave to ideals, beliefs. The inquiry into the idea of reincarnation, into the spirit world, only leads to further enslavement. All this indicates poverty of being. To cover it up, you seek guides, systems of thought. However much the mind may try to escape from that shallowness, it continues to express itself in many ways. It is important that in suffering, in bereavement, mind does not escape through any remedy, that it faces wholly its own emptiness. In becoming fully conscious you will observe how the mind is ever trying to avoid the deep understanding of the cause of sorrow. In that full awareness you will truly dissolve the cause.

Through choiceless discernment, there is awakened that creative intuition, intelligence, which alone can free the mind-heart from the many subtle processes of ignorance, want and fear. Happiness is not to be sought after, but with the cessation of sorrow, there is intelligence. Then there is joy. In it there is no duality, no sense of loss, no division.

CHAPTER 12

Conflict

*Conflict arises between the permanent and impermanent
quality of resistance. Resistance perpetuates itself through
acquisitiveness, through ignorance, through conscious and
unconscious craving for experience. What you call the
permanent is part of resistance itself, and so part of conflict.
The thing that the mind clings to as the permanent is
in its very essence the transient. It is the outcome of ignorance,
fear, craving.*

The external approach to the problem of conflict leads to the possibility of losing yourself in an ideology, in service, in the state. You hope unconsciously through your attention "out there" that your personal sorrows, anxieties, responsibilities and conflicts will disappear. And yet, in spite of the attempt to sacrifice yourself to the outer, there remains the "I" with its personal, limited ambitions, hopes, fears, passions and greed. You may give yourself to the state, but as long as the "I" remains, the state becomes the new means for your expansion, for your glory. Cunning thought will again bring about new chaos and misery. Competition and power will always be sought as long as the "I" exists. Competition is the outer manifestation of the inner conflict of ambition, envy and the worship of success.

The other approach to the problem of conflict is from *within;* to understand the many causes that create conflict in relationship, and so with society. You try to overcome one cause by another cause, one substitution by another, and so thought gets tangled in its own vicious net. You try to remove the cause of conflict and misery by assertions, by logical and rational conclusions. You worship God or an idea or a pattern in order to forget yourself and be free of your daily struggles. You have the idea that through constant assertion and control you can discipline yourself with a spiritual essence and thus escape your daily conflicts in relationship and action. Thus the pattern, the belief, becomes more important than the understanding of life.

Conflict is the impeded flow of spontaneous action, of harmonious thought and feeling. When mind and heart are in a state of discord, they create conflict. Such impediment to harmonious action is caused by the continual avoidance of facing life wholly. Life is met with the weight of tradition, be it religious, political or social. This incapacity to face experience in its completeness creates conflict, and also the desire to escape from it.

When you do not yield to false demands and stupidities, you also begin to create vital conflict. Then you will find that your family, your friends and public opinion are against you. It will create great suffering in you. It is only when you suffer and do not try to escape from that suffering, when you see that explanations are futile, when all escapes have been stopped, it is only then that you will begin to discern truly, fundamentally, deeply in your heart, what the limitations are that prevent the free flow of reality in life.

There *is* a complete answer to your problem of conflict, which is not based on dogmatism or on theories. This answer is to be found when you approach the problem integrally from the center; you must understand the process of the "I" in its relationship with another, with action, with belief. The complete solution for your conflict is in the voluntary transformation of the process of the "I," intelligently and sanely without compulsion. As most of us are unwilling to concentrate thought on the fundamental alteration in the center, legislation and institutions force us to adjust ourselves to an outer pattern, in the hope of achieving social harmony. But these outer adjustments do not eradicate the cause of conflict. Compulsion does not create understanding, whether it is from the outside or from the inside. Conflict manifests in your daily life through traditions, moral values, impositions of vested interests, attachment, acquisitiveness; these create conditions that prevent human happiness. Our lives are in continual conflict because of fear, belief, choice and subjugation. Become aware of craving in all its expressions in your daily life, how it works in your thoughts and actions. Then understanding comes without choice. Only through conflict, through suffering, through conscious action and not by discussing intellectually, can man become aware of these impediments.

If you understand the significance of environment, poverty, wealth, exploitation, oppression, nationalities, religions and all the inanities of social life in modern existence and do not try to overcome them but see their significance, then there must be individual action, and complete revolution of ideas and thought. Then there is no longer a struggle, but rather light dispelling darkness.

The cause of conflict lies in the constant battle between everchanging life and the desire of the "I" for permanency. Conflict invariably must arise when there is a static center—"you," while about you there are changing values. This static center must be in battle with the living quality of life, change. The primary cause of friction is yourself, the "I," the self that is the static center of unified craving.

Conflict can only and must inevitably exist between the false and the false. There cannot be conflict between what is true and what is false. There must be conflict between the opposites, between two false things. In conflict you have divided intelligence from mind and heart. When this happens there comes the consciousness of insufficiency. In that sense of void, you begin to seek happiness, completeness, in art, in music, in nature, in religious ideals, and so on. These begin to influence your life, to control, to dominate and guide you, and you think that in this way you will arrive at completeness.

Conflict arises between the permanent and impermanent quality of resistance. Resistance perpetuates itself through acquisitiveness, through ignorance, through conscious and unconscious craving for experience. What you call the permanent is part of resistance itself, and so part of conflict. The thing that the mind clings to as the permanent is in its very essence the transient. It is the outcome of ignorance, fear, craving.

As long as your relationship with another (be it a person, idea or thing) is possessive there must be conflict, for conflict arises when there is physiological and psychological dependence.

There is a dual process at work in us, the action of the opposites, want and not want. This conflict exists between the outgoing will to do and the will to refrain from doing.

There are two different approaches to the problem of conflict. The division is artificial, for convenience only. The one is the approach from the outside, and the other is from within. Only for the sake of clarity do we here divide life as the outer and the inner, but you must have an integrated understanding to comprehend the complex problem of life.

When we try to solve the problem of existence from the outside, as it were, we soon realize that there must be a complete social and economic change; we see that there must be the elimination of barriers, racial, notional, economic; we perceive also that we must be free of religious barriers, with their separative dogmas and beliefs, which cause different groups to be formed in antagonistic competition with each other. The outside approach indicates that emphasis must be laid on institutions, on legislation, on the importance of the state. Though the action of the state may momentarily give satisfactory results, there is inherent in it great possibilities of corruption and brutality. For the sake of an ideology, man will sacrifice man.

Disharmony is the result of the consciousness divided between what we think and what we feel. In that distinction there is conflict. To think and feel is the same, they are one. Conflict and disharmony is the struggle between the "I" consciousness, the instrument of disharmony and the environment itself, the media of disharmony.

The lack of understanding of environment, of our surroundings, creates disharmony. When we begin to question and understand environment, its full worth and significance, not try to imitate or follow it or adjust ourselves to it or escape from it, then there is born intelligence, then there is harmony.

Division arises from the constant resistance of man to the continual change of values. Our whole effort is concerned with the superimposition of what we call right ideas or what we call wrong ideas. By this attempt we continually create division in action. We do not understand that choice born of want, emptiness, fear, the craving to be certain, is the cause of division.

All reforms in religion, in moral standards, in social life and political organizations merely dictate adjustment to ever-changing environment. Through this ever-increasing conflict, divisions and sects are created. Each mind creates a new set of values according to its own reactions to the environment. Then begins the division of peoples, class distinctions and fierce antagonisms between creeds, between doctrines, between states. Out of the immensity of this conflict arise experts, calling themselves reformers in religion and healers of social and economic ills. So blinded are they by their own expertise, that they manage only to increase division and struggle. These religious reformers, social reformers and political reformers, all experts in their own limitations, are all dividing our life and human functioning into compartments and conflicts.

This division, brought about by the reliance upon experts, is nothing but the laziness of your mind, so that you need not think but merely conform. So mind becomes increasingly bound,

120

enslaved and divided. So long as mind has not understood the significance of environment, there will be divisions.

Life cannot be divided. We cannot think we are going to change and yet be a nationalist; we can't be class-conscious and yet talk about brotherhood, or create walls around our particular country and yet talk about the unity of life. Yet this is what we are doing all the time. You are possessive, nationalistic and class-conscious, and yet divide that separative consciousness from your "spiritual" consciousness in which you try to be brotherly, follow ethics, morality and try to realize God. You have divided life into compartments.

Man isolates himself from his fellow man by following the process of craving. His self-centered, egotistical, competitive, action divides, separates him from his fellow men. Isolation is possible only in a state of neurosis.

CHAPTER 13

Mistaken Identities

To understand yourself, your self-identification, there must be constant awareness. Awareness will bring to the surface the causes of violence and hatred, greed and ambition. By studying them without identification, they will be transcended. The more you are aware of your thought-feelings, the more you become detached. And the less you identify, the greater the self-knowledge. It is this self-knowledge that dissolves ignorance and sorrow.

Through contact, sensation, and perception you have an experience, which gives you either pleasure or pain. You want pleasure, you don't want pain. This constant change of want and not want gives you a personal identity, the "I." It forms the identification of "you" and "me." This constant acceptance and rejection not only creates the "I" but establishes it as memory. Then want or craving, through memory, creates and maintains the self, the me and mine.

You are a collection of memories, innumerable memories of experience, which you have gathered through life, and the "I" is the result of identification with them all.

You are the result of identifying yourself with a particular nation, whether American, Dutch, German, Indian, etc.

You are the result of identifying yourself with a particular race, with a particular country, with a religion. You are identified with all that you possess, all that you think and feel. This conditioning is the identification process.

To identify yourself with a particular race, with a particular country, with a class, with certain ideologies, gives security, satisfaction and self-importance. Identification is with the part, not the whole. The worship of the part instead of the whole results in division, conflict and confusion. In identifying yourself with what you consider to be the greater, you yourself hope to become greater. But you still remain as you are. It is only the label that has changed.

You feel lost without identification with a group, a house, a plan, an organization, a religion or a non-religion, property, money, with an idea, with a person. You cling to memory, to identification, because it gives you continuity.

The "I" process is the process of identification. The "I" seeks to exploit, to be acquisitive, to be possessive in love, ideas and things. The "I" process begins and continues in identification with its own self-created limitations. Identification prevents the flow of thought-feeling. It implies acceptance or denial, judgment or comparison. Understanding ceases if there is identification.

When living by this duality process, anything of the outer environment that man accepts and uses, or rejects or discards, and anything that he creates on the inner, as a reaction to the outer, are the means of identification. And also, all that he expresses arising from these acquired responses, or self-developed reactions of the inner, identifies him in his consciousness as being that which is expressed.

Through identification man establishes continuity of the static center as the self. Man remains in constant identification as the "I," the "me," in which the method of identification may undergo change, but identification and the process of identification never varies.

If you are to have understanding, then identification must cease. There must be awareness without identification. There cannot be freedom, liberation from the self, if identification continues. Hence, the main barrier to understanding is this constant achieving, grasping, holding on to the substance of experience, and your identification with it.

As long as you live in psychological identification, you will be an imitator, an intellectual parrot, a machine and slave to all that is in you and about you.

In becoming aware of your process of the self, with its accumulative memory, the psychological instrument of identification, you will begin to understand its time-binding quality, the craving for continual identification. It is this time-binding quality of the self with its identifying memory that must be studied, understood and so transcended.

The clarification of the superficial layers comes when thought-feeling is not identifying, but capable of observing without comparison and judgment. If you do not identify, then as thought-feeling flows, follow it through, think it out, feel it out, clearly and intelligently, not the stimulus, the challenge, but your response to it. Then order and clarity will come into that thin layer of consciousness.

To understand yourself, your self-identification, there must be constant awareness. Awareness will bring to the surface the causes of violence and hatred, greed and ambition. By studying them without identification, they will be transcended.

The more you are aware of your thought-feelings, the more you become detached. And the less you identify, the greater the self-knowledge. It is this self-knowledge that dissolves ignorance and sorrow.

CHAPTER 14

Conditioning

Blessedness is ever in the present, and to experience it requires constant interest and awareness. Peace is in the present, but to understand it one must not be concerned with time. Blessedness is not a reward. One has to be alert, aware, in a state of continual understanding, never letting one thought or word pass by without seeing its significance. This state of awareness is happiness.

Action based on limitation, ignorance, arises each moment. It modifies and renews the "I" process, giving it continuity and identity. This continuity of action through limitation is commonly thought of as predestination. It is actually the result of cause and effect. Cause and effect exist together. They are a joint phenomenon not to be separated. Though the effect may take time to come into being, the seed of effect is in the cause, it coexists with the cause. It is no longer cause and effect but a much more subtle, delicate problem to be thought out, to be experienced. It is the problem of conditioning, which causes predestination. Cause and effect become the means of conditioning consciousness. You are, by your own acts, being conditioned.

But at any moment you can break this chain of limitation. You are a free agent at all times. You are not the plaything of some entity, some mysterious force, good or evil. You are not at the mercy of some erratic forces in the world. You need not be controlled by heredity and environment. If the mind is cognizant of the process of ignorance, this conditioning process, it can be free of it at any moment. If you deeply comprehend this, you will see that thought need not ever be conditioned by cause and effect.

The concept of the soul divides life. There is the body, then there is the soul that occupies it, and finally there is God or reality. The concept of the soul has been created through our desire for immortality. You think that there must be some other entity, which is more spiritual than this body. And so you divide life into the soul, the permanent, and the body, the transient. This division creates illusion.

If the soul is spiritual essence, above and beyond all physical and psychological conditioning, apart from this thing called the "I," then the "I" is of no importance. And also, if that spiritual entity, the soul, is in us, if it cannot be contaminated, if nothing can be added to it, then why do we exert ourselves to understand? Then why do we cling to the "I" so desperately? Why are we caught in its perpetuity, in its expansive desires, in its ambitions and achievements? If this spiritual essence is supposed to be love, intelligence, truth, then how can it be surrounded by this feverish pursuit of the demands of the self?

So when we say there is a spiritual entity, a soul, surely this is an illusion, a belief. We have accepted this idea because it is very gratifying, comforting.

What is the soul that you call immortal? What are you? A form, a name, with certain prejudices, qualities, hopes and fears. What is this "I"? It is the limited consciousness, the end product of limited action, creating its own illusions, and caught in its own ignorance. You believe this "I" to be reality.

But reality or truth or God or whatever the name you give it, is not egotistic, personal consciousness. Having created the soul, you ask, "Is it immortal?" When mind is free from its limited consciousness, with its desire for continuance, then there is immortality, not of personal, individual continuance, but of life itself.

Whether spirits exist or not is not of importance, but let us consider the desire, the belief in spirits that prompts you to communicate with them. The desire is for guidance, for direction, in order that you may not make mistakes and suffer. Also, one very gratifying thing is that the dead cannot contradict you. You use anything and everything in order to have security, so spirits to whom you have accredited divine wisdom come in for their share of your search of assurance, gain.

Ceremony is glorified sensation. With religious ceremonial as with worldly pomp, when a king holds court, the spectators are tremendously impressed and greatly exploited.

In a religious ceremony you either hope to advance spiritually through its efficacy or you attend it in order to spread spiritual forces in the hope of gaining spiritual advancement.

When you think you are spreading spiritual force in the world, how do you know you are doing this? Either it must be based on authority, acceptance of someone else's edict or precepts, or you feel that you yourself are spreading it.

If someone else says "do that," and you do it, then it has no value; it does not matter who authorizes it. Then you reduce yourself to becoming the instrument of authority. Therefore there is no validity in your actions.

You might, by attending church, feel elated, feel full of vitality and a sense of well-being. You feel the same after taking a drink or attending a stimulating lecture. Why do you place ceremony as being more important, more vital, more essential?

You hope by attending a ceremony, by some miraculous process your whole being will be cleansed.

Such ideas are instruments of exploitation. This whole concept that ceremonies are going to give you spiritual understanding and attainment is really the same thing that every materialistic person thinks. He wants to be somebody in this world, he wants to have money, so he begins to accumulate, possess, exploit, to be ruthless; and the man who wants to be somebody in the spiritual world does exactly the same thing, only he calls it spiritual.

Behind it all, there is the idea of gain; and such an idea, the desire to attain, is in itself a limitation. If you perform ceremonies as a means of gain, then all ceremonies are but a limitation. Or if you perform ceremonies as essential, as necessary, then you are merely accepting it on authority or tradition.

There is another aspect of ceremony—the idea that in

ceremony lies magic—not white and black magic, but that the mystery of life is unfolded through ceremony. There is something immense, magical about life; but you cannot experience it through spurious, unnatural things. All ceremonies are unessential for the fulfillment of life.

Hope is the outcome of the present, influenced by the past, in regard to the future. Hope for the future implies postponement of the present. To look to the future for hope is to create delusion. Life is in the present. It can never be in the future.

People, in their desire for happiness, have tried everything—one thing after another. They abandon that which does not satisfy them one satisfaction to the other. First, they think that they will find happiness in the possession of material goods and in pleasure. If they do not find it in these, they turn their desires toward so-called spiritual ends. They hope to find these in a world that they believe real, but which is created by hope and their own fantasy. In this unreal world beliefs of all kinds, religions, occultism and mysticism are to be found.

In searching, going from one belief to another, people are basing their life on hope. To the degree to which one's search is based on the hope of finding comfort, of finding balm for one's wounds, by that extent one moves away from reality, truth. Truth has no need for prayer, or adoration, or religion, or rites. It is absolute. Anyone can find truth if he is deeply aware of his daily actions, his thoughts and his emotions. Hope is the betrayal of truth, for it pins a man to a future expectancy and removes him further from the present.

If you really want to help man because you yourself perceive the utter chaos and suffering that exists, you will not give him any drug that will put him to sleep. You will help him to discover for himself those causes that impede the birth of intelligence. If you can help another to be aware, that is all that you need to do. But that is the most difficult thing, for intelligence does not offer shelter from struggle and the turmoil of life, nor does it give comfort. It only creates understanding. You can help another to free himself only when you begin to free yourself. But you have this extraordinary attitude of wanting to improve the masses while you yourself are ignorant, still caught in superstition, in acquisitiveness. When you begin to free yourself, then you will help another naturally, without trying.

Whether you are exploiting or not depends on what you mean by "helping" and "spreading happiness." Everybody wants to help, especially those who belong to sects, organized religions, charitable organizations, etc. It is a disease, because they think that by doing something, it does not matter what, they are going to help. You can "help" another and so enslave him, or you can help another to understand himself. You can spread happiness by encouraging illusion, by giving superficial comfort and security, which appear to be lasting. Or you can help another to discern the many illusions in which he is caught. If you are capable of the latter kind of help, then you are not exploiting.

Who is to say what service is? For example, a man who belongs to the army and is prepared to kill the enemy, says that he is serving his country. The man who kills another to save the world says he is serving the world, God. The man who kills animals, the butcher, says he is serving the community. The industrialist who controls the means of production says he is serving the country, the community. The priest who blesses mankind and preaches brotherhood blesses men who go off to kill. He says he is serving his country, humanity, God. Who is to decide?

Or should you look at it quite differently? Do you think a flower, a rose, would consider it is serving humanity, that it is helping the world by its existence, because it is beautiful? On the contrary, because it is beautiful, unconscious of its own loveliness, it is truly helping. Each of you use your methods or your ideas to exploit the world, not to set the world free. To really help, you must be free from that limited consciousness, the "I," the ego. So long as that exists, you are not serving. Unless you really deeply think about this you cannot find out if you are truly helping.

We can help man to have a creative purpose, to attain that freedom that is essential for all. It is not enough to make industry produce more and more things, to make workers comfortable, to give them leisure, if they are still bound by their limitations. Desires should be utilized to make man free, not to improve the prison of our so-called civilization.

The cultivation of respect, the organization of phrases, is not culture, it is but a trap to hold the thoughtless. Our minds have become so caught in habitual values that we have lost all affection and deep respect for human life. Where there is exploitation there can be no respect for human dignity.

The show of respect to those in authority or the aged is generally a habit. Fear can assume the form of veneration. There is no respect for the aged, as such, but only the respect for authority and the habit of fear. Love cannot become a habit.

True respect is not shown only to the one or the few, but to all. Your show of respect to the one or the few, only indicates a mentality of barter. You expect to get something, and so you show respect. What you are really doing is showing respect to a person who may help you. Out of this false respect there is born contempt for others. This is indeed a reciprocal exploitation. The mere respect for authority indicates fear, which breeds many illusions; from this false respect there arises the artificial distinction between leaders and followers, with its many obvious and subtle forms of exploitation. Where there is no intelligence, there is respect for the one or the few and disdain for the rest.

True respect is born of understanding. It is not concerned with gain. Living in the moment is true respect.

A man whose heart and mind are closed can only have love for a few; such a man demands friends, because he relies on them for his comfort, consolation, satisfaction. When real friendship exists, there will not be discrimination for the few. Relationship will be fulfilled equally with all.

Tolerance is a clever invention of your mind. Tolerance merely indicates the desire to cling to your own idiosyncrasies, your own limited ideas and prejudices, and allow another to pursue his own. In tolerance there is not intelligent diversity, but only a kind of superior indifference. It is an intellectual invention to keep you where you are and to keep me where I am, and try to be friendly. Its action causes us to compromise with the issues of life. The cultivation of tolerance is only an intellectual fear and so is without significance. It leads to thoughtlessness and poverty of being. Tolerance always implies a sense of superiority.

Understanding and love are of primary importance, virtues are of secondary importance. Duty, courage, charity as virtues are in the likeness of their opposites. They may be misused and become a source of grave danger. Take for example duty, as a virtue—this can be and is being brutally and tragically misused. Without understanding and love, virtues can become the instruments of barbarity and cruelty.

Men have raised within themselves a double barrier to truth; wealth and poverty. But truth cannot be found by means of spiritual or material possessions, or the rejection of possessions. It is not the result of compensations in these fields. Truth is neither rich nor poor.

The rich man who decides to be poor and gives away all his possessions, accomplishes an action that is equal to zero. It is not an action, in the real sense of the word, but a reaction. Poverty for him is merely the opposite of wealth, within a conflict that has not been resolved. It is as erroneous to believe that wealth is evil and poverty is a virtue, as it is to believe the opposite. Wealth is possession. Poverty is a lack of possession. Both are negative. When wealth and poverty are outside of all possessiveness, they acquire in that detachment a new meaning. Your lack of psychological complications becomes your wealth.

Philanthropy is the returning of a little to the victim from whom it has been expropriated. It is egotism. The only true philanthropy is to help a man to realize that in his own hands lies his happiness and the welfare of the whole.

Courage as a virtue is false. Do not seek to be courageous, but let the mind be free of fear. Understand that courage is but an escape from fear, so see the futility of seeking it.

Habit is conscious or unconscious repetition of action, which is guided by memory of past incidents, of tradition, of thought-desire patterns, and so forth. For most of you action is habit, and this gives your actions an apparent continuity. Almost always it is habit that rules your actions and relationships.

Fear, the search for security, is the root of this habit-forming mechanism and habit is of the mind of the will. Habit merely conceals fear without doing away with it.

Where there is habit, the following of patterns or ideals, pliability is impossible. To be pliable requires constant awareness, and as the mind finds it easier to establish patterns than to be aware, it proceeds to form habits. When shaken from a particular habit, through conflict and uncertainty, it moves to another habit. Fear for its own security and comfort compels the mind to follow thought-desire patterns. Society thus becomes the maker of habit, patterns, ideals.

Sometimes you realize that you are living in a narrow groove of thought, but breaking away from it, you slip into another. Unfortunately you reduce all contact with each other to a dull and weary pattern through incapacity of adjustment. This causes fear, through the lack of love.

In trying to escape from ignorance and fear, you form habits, habits of ideals and morality. When there is discontentment, sorrow, the intellect mechanically comes forward with solutions, explanations, tentative suggestions, which gradually crystallize and become habits of thought. Thus suffering and doubt are covered over. To understand this mechanism of escape through habit, you must find out the concealed motive, the motive that drives you to a certain action, which you call experience.

Habit gradually overcomes thinking. Observe the activity of your own mind, your own thought, and you will see how it is forming itself into one habit after another. The conscious is thus becoming the unconscious. Habit hardens the mind through will and discipline. Forcing the mind to discipline itself, through fear, brings about frustration. Outside influences and inward determinations do not break the formation or habit, but only aid in superficial and intellectual adjustment, which is not conducive to true relationship.

If action is the outcome of mere mechanical habit, then it must lead to confusion and sorrow. If relationship is merely the contact between two individual habits, then all such relationship is suffering (as so often in marriage). All true relationship requires constant alertness, pliability and adjustment.

What is prayer? Is it not an appeal based on self-desire, a concept that you can make supplication to some supernatural power for benefits on your behalf, regardless of whether you merit them or not? The fundamental idea of prayer is to seek aid and understanding from beyond yourself.

Most people indulge in petitionary prayer. However you may petition, your answer will be according to your demand. It will not be real. The answer to a desire is in the desire itself. When you ask out of greed, out of fear, out of want, you will have an answer. but you must pay for it. Greed replies to greed. When you ask you may receive but you will have to pay for it in ways you did not expect. The centuries of greed and ignorance manifest themselves when you call upon them.

For many centuries man has been guided through fear, forced, compelled to act according to certain standards; but the highest form of morality is to do a thing for its own sake, not for a motive or for a reward. Now, instead of being coerced to follow a pattern, we have to find out individually what is true morality. This is one of the most difficult things to do, to find out for oneself how to act truly; it demands great intelligence, a continual adjustment, not the following of a law or a system. To act with true morality, there must be an intense awareness, discernment, in the moment of action itself. And this can be only when the mind is liberating itself from fear and compulsions.

Do not make what you call the ascetic life the highest purpose. That is a very small detail. True asceticism is not the deification of primitivism. By becoming primitive, by suppressing, you may think that you are going to realize truth. The ascetic is detached in whatever circumstance he may find himself. But to be a true ascetic, you must be very honest, otherwise you can deceive yourself hopelessly, as many do. You need the integrity of thought and the clarity of purpose that will lead you to a life of utter detachment—not of indifference, but detachment with affection, with enthusiasm. If you give your thought, your life, your reason, your whole substance to it, you will understand. Asceticism generally comes from the desire to escape, from the fear of experience. But you must be absolutely detached with comprehension. There is no renunciation. Where there is no understanding, there is renunciation. If you are really detached, which needs comprehension of right value of experience, then you are free inwardly and outwardly; outwardly as far as your environment permits, but inwardly assuredly.

Blessedness is ever in the present, and to experience it requires constant interest and awareness. Peace is in the present, but to understand it one must not be concerned with time. Blessedness is not a reward. One has to be alert, aware, in a state of continual understanding, never letting one thought or word pass by without seeing its significance. This state of awareness is happiness.

Faith is created by fear. Faith, or acceptance, is a hindrance to the deep comprehension of life. Included in the word faith are the many subtle demands, prayers and supplications to an external being, whether he be a master or a saint; or there is the appeal to the authority of beliefs, ideals and self-imposed disciplines. Having such a faith, with all its implications, you are bound to create duality in life; that is, there is the actor trying to approximate himself and his actions to a concept, a standard, to a belief, to an ideal.

CHAPTER 15

Emptiness

*Emptiness results when action (reaction) is born of choice.
Emptiness is action born of choice, in search of gain. Emptiness
is poverty of being, shallowness, insufficiency, incompleteness,
loneliness. When the mind is conscious of its incompleteness it
tries to escape from it and therefore creates an opposite.*

Man's present psychological manner of living, based on psychological reaction, is inadequate, illusory, futile and empty. It always creates conflict, wars and suffering. It is a self-evident fact that the means we are using to experience life are erroneous. As the means consist of man's way of thinking, feeling and acting, which is his consciousness, it is apparent where the error lies.

Man is his consciousness. His consciousness is the means by and through which he meets life. We cannot set him apart from it, nor can we deny it as being the vital element through which he acts. To live, he uses that which he is. He uses himself to fulfill himself psychologically.

Psychologically acquired and conditioned consciousness, that consciousness which is in constant search for security, for pleasure and the avoidance of pain, is not adequate to solve the problems of life.

Man is empty of the means whereby he can live in understanding with his fellow man. He will remain so, and his life will continue to be as it is, if he continues to use his present methods of thinking, feeling and acting. His reactionary way of life is empty. It is the "I," the "I" consciousness, the "I" process. This entire process of the search for the fulfillment of pleasure, self-gratification, is emptiness itself. It never fulfills, it never sustains, it never brings peace, serenity, understanding. It results in constant conflict, sorrow and suffering. All "I" action is empty action—it has no intrinsic value. It requires constant and continual expression to gain a small measure of joy, which for the most part is simply sensation.

Emptiness results when action (reaction) is born of choice. Emptiness is action born of choice, in search of gain.

Emptiness is poverty of being, shallowness, insufficiency, incompleteness, loneliness. When the mind is conscious of its incompleteness it tries to escape from it and therefore creates an opposite.

You need to understand that where there is incompleteness, emptiness, there is the desire for guidance, for authority, for an influence that can act as a guide. When you become conscious of that emptiness you desire to fill it and look for a pattern that another has established, hoping that it will fill the emptiness, the shallowness of which you have become more and more conscious.

You begin to live, not with your own experience, within your own understanding, but with the expression, the ideas, the limitations of another's experience. You begin to gather and accumulate, hoping to become complete through this gathering of experiences or things and the enjoyment of other people's ideas or patterns. Or when you feel empty, lonely, you create standards, ideals to sustain you in your emptiness. They become your external authority.

Where there is insufficiency, emptiness, there must be compulsion; and out of this compulsion is born a particular method of action, which creates further pain. Where you consciously or unconsciously feel the poignancy of insufficiency, there must be conflict and a sense of shallowness and emptiness and the utter futility of life.

So you look to action, dissipation of this insufficiency; you are not trying to find out what the cause of insufficiency is. You are trying to fill this void, this loneliness, this incompleteness through sensation, excitement or pleasure, through tenderness or forgetfulness. You seek and crave enrichment through possessions or you try to seek it in relationship or in ideas.

But you can never fill the void, for your action is based on attraction and repulsion, like and dislike. You are creating an opposite, creating duality. Your action to choose a way out is born of want and fear, conditioned by attraction and repulsion. That is your whole life.

As long as you choose between opposites, there is no discernment and so choice and effort are ceaseless and continuous. Your action is always in terms of achievement or escape from pain, and therefore that emptiness that you feel will always exist. Emptiness is action born of choice, in search of gain. Emptiness results and remains when action is born of choice. But the mind is free of choice, when it has the capacity to discern; then action is infinite. As soon as you cease to choose, emptiness ceases.

Poverty of being is revealed when you try to overcome emptiness, shallowness by covering it up with possessions, with the worship of success, and virtues. Then things, property, come to have great significance; then class, social position, country, pride of race assume great importance, and have to be maintained at all costs; then name, family and their continuance become vital. Or, if you try to cover up this emptiness with ideas, beliefs, creeds, fancies, then opinion, goodwill and the experience of others take on powerful importance; then ceremonies, priests, masters, saviors, become essential and they destroy self-reliance; then authority is worshipped. Thus the fear of what one is, psychological emptiness, creates an action, which is really a reaction born of choice in search of gain, which is a continuation of the process of emptiness, so again it results in emptiness, illusion, uncertainty.

So long as there is craving, desire, want, there must be painful insufficiency, emptiness. Without understanding the process of desire, the cause, you try to deal with the effect, insufficiency, and get lost in its intricacies.

Whereas if you become aware through action, have awareness,

then you will find out the cause of insufficiency, incompleteness.

Become aware of the fallacy of accumulative sufficiency then thought begins to free itself from those possessions that it has accumulated for itself through fear of incompleteness. Understand the functioning of your thought and your own emotion, and so in that action become aware. Then there is intelligence that dispels insufficiency, incompleteness. Completeness, wholeness is not the aggregation of many parts or the expansion of the self. It is to be realized through understanding and love. Where there is completeness, there cannot be compulsion, only intelligence, which is thought and emotion in perfect harmony.

Self-perpetuation is the basic purpose of man. Continual self-perpetuation is the most basic action of man.

Man's present purpose is his search for security, certainty, continuity. Each individual is seeking security, certainty, both subjectively and objectively. His search is for certainty, that the mind can cling to it, undisturbed. And his objective search is for security, power and well-being. Thought being uncertain, fearful, creates and clings to certainties, definite results and achievements, either those of someone it considers great or its own assured memories. Thought moves from the known to the known, from one certainty to another certainty, from one assurance to another. It fulfills all its action through pleasure and gain, the basic determinants of physio-psychological reaction to experience.

You base all your action on pleasure and pain, like and dislike, attraction and repulsion. This is your mental and emotional reaction to all experience. The mind is caught up in its response to pleasure and pain. When an experience gives you pain and, at the same time, gives you pleasure, you do nothing about it. You act only when the pain is greater than the pleasure, but if the pleasure is the greater, you do nothing at all about it, because there is no acute conflict. It is only when the pain overbalances pleasure, is more acute than pleasure, than you demand action.

CHAPTER 16

Values

*So how is one to awaken intelligence? What happens in
moments of great crisis? In that rich moment when memory is
not present, in that acute, intense awareness of the circumstance,
of the environment, there is perception of what is true. You have
this perception in moments of crisis. You are fully conscious of
all circumstances, of the condition about you. You are also aware
that mind cannot find the answer. In that intensely acute crisis,
intelligence functions and there is spontaneous understanding.*

Even in times of peace and quiet, in times of settled comfort, a gradual transformation of values continually takes place. It is commonly called the struggle between the values of the old generation and the new, the struggle between the old and the young. It is the continual battle that takes place between the settled, comfortable, stagnating mind and new circumstances that are forcing the old mind into facing new conditions so that it has to create a new set of values.

In times of upheaval and great conflict, violent and ruthless changes in values take place. These swift, violent, ruthless changes we call revolution.

Let us examine what values really are. Are they fundamental? Is it possible for the mind to act intelligently, spontaneously, naturally, without imparting values? Wherever there is dissatisfaction with environment, with circumstances, that discontent leads to the desire for change, reform. What you call reform is the destruction of the old and the creation of a new set of values.

Circumstances change slowly or rapidly, and the creation of a new set of values is the result of adjustments to ever-changing environment. Values are merely the pattern of conformity. Why should you have values? Aren't they a mold, established by yourself or society, to which the mind, in its laziness, in its lack of perception desires to conform? Mind seeks a certainty, a conclusion, and in that search acts; or it has trained itself to develop a background and from that background it functions. Or it has a belief, and from that belief it colors its activities. Mind demands values so that it will not be at a loss, so that it will always have a guide to follow, to imitate. So values become molds in which mind stagnates. Even the purpose of education is to compel the mind and heart to conform to the prevailing values of society.

So all changes in religion, in oral standards, in social life and political organizations are the dictates of desire for adjustment to ever-changing environment. This is called reform. Environments are constantly changing, circumstances are continually in movement, and values are changed accordingly. These new values are glorified as being fundamental, original, true. Actually, they are only new forms of conformity; subtle forms of modification. The new values help to bring about piecemeal reformation, a transformation of cloaks, which we call progress.

Freedom is not going from an old mold into a new one, from an old stupidity into a new stupidity, or from revolting against tradition to embrace the license of mindlessness. And yet you will observe that those people who talk a great deal about freedom, liberation, are doing just that. They have put away their old tradition and have now a pattern of their own to which they conform. Conformity is the absence of intelligence. What you call tradition is merely outer environment with its values, and what you call freedom from tradition is but enslavement to some inner environment and its values. In any case that is merely adjustment, not comprehension, of environment. From this there arises, naturally, the question whether the mind can ever discover any lasting values, so that there will not be this constant change, this constant conflict created by new values.

We are very accustomed to values and their continual change. What we call the essentials soon become unessential. In this continual change of values lies conflict. As long as we do not fundamentally understand the change of values, and the cause of that change, we shall always be caught up in the wheel of conflicting values.

We need to understand that at present our whole life is movement from value to value; from essential to essential, from merit to merit, from reward to reward, from gain to gain, from idea to idea, from known to known, from substitution to substitution, from assurance to assurance, from one security to another. This constant changing is but an adjustment to the ever-changing environment. And thus the mind is never still, it is ever wandering, ever pursuing.

Our action consists of approximation to a memory, a pattern, a mold, a past experience. Mind is ever measuring itself against a standard or an opinion. Thought is occupied with approximation, with achievement, with success, so it is no longer capable of true discernment. This desire to gain, to attain, springs from fear, which presents true perception.

Now through economics, now through religion, now through science, man seeks to bring about order and true harmony in human life. As an individual you are making an effort to acquire virtues, pleasure, possessions and are developing toward greater accumulation and security. If you are not doing this, you go about it negatively by denying these things and trying to develop another series of subtle self-protections. Consciousness, the mind, is ever isolating itself through acquisitive and self-protective desires.

What are changing values? They are cultivated fears. There must be a change of values so long as there are essentials and unessentials, so long as there are opposites. They are created with the idea and the great worship of success, in which you include gain and achievement. The mind is pursuing them as its aim, its goal. This results in changing values, and therefore conflict.

What is it that creates changing values? Mind, which is also heart, is clouded by psychological memories. It is ever undergoing change, modifying and altering itself. It is depending ever on the movement of circumstances. As long as mind is clouded by this kind of memory, which is the outcome of adjustment to environment, and not the understanding of environment, that memory must come between intelligence and environment, and therefore there cannot be the full comprehension of environment. This memory, which you call mind, is giving and imparting values. That is the function of memory. Mind, instead of being what its true nature is, intelligence, direct perception, is clouded by psychological memory, and is giving values as true and false, essentials and unessentials, according to its cunning, according to its calculated fears and its search for security. That is the whole function of psychological memory. To the majority of people, mind is merely a machine, a storehouse of memories, which is continually giving values to the things it meets, to experiences.

Though there is no such thing as fundamental security, psychological mind seeks security after security, certainty after certainty, essential after essential, achievement after achievement. As the mind is constantly seeking certainty, the moment it has security, it regards what it has left behind as unessential. Again it is only imparting values, and thus in this process of movement from goal to goal, from essential to essential, in the process of this constant movement, its values are changing, colored by its own security and anxiety for perpetuation. So mind is caught up in the struggle of changing values, and this battle is called progress, the evolutionary path of choices leading to truth. Mind seeking security moves on and again begins to give new values to all things in its path. This process of movement you call growth, the evolutionary path of choice between the essential and the unessential.

This growth is but memory conforming and adjusting itself to its own creation, which is the environment. Fundamentally there is no difference between that memory and the environment.

Action is always the result of calculation when it is born of this conformity and adjustment. The unclear mind directed by memory is the result of the lack of understanding of environment. Such a mind must, in action, seek an escape, a culmination, a motive, and therefore that action is never free. It is always limited and is always creating further bondage, further conflict. So this vicious circle of psychological memory, burdened by its conflicts, becomes a creator of values. Environment is created by values and mind and heart become the slaves of this environment.

How is one to free the mind from giving values at all? When mind imparts values, it can only impart them out of its memory, and therefore cannot understand the full significance of environment. If I examine or try to understand circumstances through my various deep-rooted prejudices—national, racial, social or religious prejudices—how can I understand environment? Yet that is what mind attempts to do; the mind that acts from psychological memory.

Intelligence imparts no values, for values are but the measure, standards or calculations born out of protectiveness. So how is there to be this intelligence, the mirror of truth, in which there are only absolute reflections and no perversions?

How is one to have this intelligence, which destroys struggle and conflict, which brings to an end the ceaseless effort that wears out the mind itself? When you make an effort you are like a piece of wood that is being whittled away continually until there is no wood left at all. So if there is this continual effort, this constant wear, mind ceases to be itself. Effort only exists so long as there is conformity and adjustment. Whereas if there is immediate perception, immediate, spontaneous understanding of environment, there is no effort to adjust oneself.

150

So how is one to awaken this intelligence? What happens in moments of great crisis? In that rich moment when memory is not present, in that acute, intense awareness of the circumstance, of the environment, there is perception of what is true. You have this perception in moments of crisis. You are fully conscious of all circumstances, of the condition about you. You are also aware that mind cannot find the answer. In that intensely acute crisis, intelligence functions and there is spontaneous understanding.

What is it that we call a crisis, a sorrow or suffering? When the mind is lethargic, when it has gone to sleep, when it has conditioned itself to contentment, in stagnation, there suddenly comes an experience to awaken you, and that awakening, that shock, you call a crisis. Now if that crisis or conflict is really intense, then you will see in that state of acuteness of mind and heart that there is an immediate perception. That intensity ceases when memory comes in with its calculations, modifications.

Do experiment with this. Each one of us has moments of crisis. They occur very often; if one is aware they occur every minute. Now in that crisis, in that conflict, observe it, without the desire to overcome it. Then you will see that mind has understood instantaneously the cause of conflict, and in that understanding there is the dissolution of the cause. But you have so trained the mind to escape from crisis, to let memory cloud the mind, that it is very difficult to become intensely aware. Hence you seek means and ways of escape. Intelligence functions spontaneously if the mind ceases to escape, ceases to seek solutions. So when the mind is not imparting values, when there is spontaneous understanding of the crisis, which is the inner and outer environment, then there is the action of intelligence, which is freedom.

CHAPTER 17

Ideals

*Happiness is creative thinking; and creative thinking is the
infinite movement of thought, emotion and action. When
thought, which is emotion, which is action itself, is unimpeded
in its movement, is not compelled or influenced or bound by an
idea, and does not proceed from the background of tradition or
habit, then that movement is creative. Then there is happiness.
The state of awareness is happiness.*

Why do we have ideals? They may contain truths but why do we want them? We have ideals because as we cannot understand the present, the everyday existence with its cruelties, sorrow and ugliness, we want ideals to steer us through life. Without a standard, a measure, an ideal, we cannot guide ourselves through the constant battles and struggles of life. We want a standard by which to judge our actions.

What does this indicate? We establish ideals as a means of escape from the present. All ideals are a hope of alleviating suffering. But they do not, they cannot, possibly explain the reason why we are suffering.

Mind must be free to understand the conflicts, the troubles, the suffering as they are. At times, when you are really in great conflict, great suffering, at that moment you are not thinking of an ideal, of what you should or should not do. You are so consumed by suffering that you want to find out. It is only when suffering diminishes, quietens down, that you turn to an ideal to help you.

You will see that you have innumerable ideals, many beliefs, and according to those you are trying to live. Now if you realize fundamentally what is real, what facts are and recognize their significance, then you will find out the very root of your escapes. You will free yourself from these false standards, false measurements, which are constantly trying to shape your mind to a particular pattern.

You have established your religious ideals, which are really your securities, in order to maintain those ideals. You have particular ways of conduct, practices, ceremonies and beliefs. You say, "I shall pursue virtue; I shall act in this way or that way in order to find happiness; I shall find out that truth is in order to overcome confusion, misery; I shall serve in order to have the blessings of heaven." This attitude toward action as a means of future acquisition is constantly crippling your thought. In trying to carry out your ideals, there arise schisms, sects, cults, creeds. You have your beliefs, and another has his; yet you all talk of brotherly love, tolerance and unity.

Ideals are false. Your mind is so crippled, so burdened with ideals that you cannot see clearly the actual. So free the mind of your ideals, which are but frustrated hopes; then only will you be capable of discerning the present with all its significance. Instead of escaping, act in the present. That action uncovers reality, which no ideal can reveal.

Happiness is creative thinking; and creative thinking is the infinite movement of thought, emotion and action. When thought, which is emotion, which is action itself, is unimpeded in its movement, is not compelled or influenced or bound by an idea, and does not proceed from the background of tradition or habit, then that movement is creative. Then there is happiness. The state of awareness is happiness.

Peace is within and not without. There can only be peace and happiness in the world when the individual, who is the world, alters the causes within himself that produce confusion, sorrow, hate. Peace is not a thing to be achieved from the outside; it can only come from within. It requires great earnestness and concentration to understand the complex problem of peace.

The man whose mind is burdened with fear, tradition, ideals, racial loyalties, such a man is dutiful. Such a mind coming into contact with the movement of life only creates friction and suffering for itself.

There is no such thing as equality among men.

You profess the ideal of brotherly love, and that is the ideal with which many of you have been brought up. But what is actually taking place? There is the distinction of classes, religions with their contrary beliefs, dogmas and divisions, and nationalism with its exploitation and wars. So of what good are your ideals? They become drugs, which prevent you from thinking clearly and from understanding what you are really doing.

Character becomes a limitation if it is merely egotistical defense against life. This development of resisting the movement of life becomes a means of self-protection. In this there cannot be intelligence, and action which only creates further limitation and sorrow. We have developed a system in which, to live at all, we must possess what is known as character, which is but a carefully cultivated resistance, a self-defense against life.

Character is the power to resist the many encroachments of society upon us. It results from the use of the will.

A man who would live, fulfill, must have intelligence. Character is merely a hindrance, a limitation, and in its development there cannot be fulfillment. The "man of character" is no nearer truth than the man without character. Each is held in his own self-consciousness, and self-consciousness is the very opposite of truth. One must be free of both character and the lack of character. Neither the man of virtue nor the man of sin is near truth, but he is near who is free of both.

CHAPTER 18

Effort

*Right effort means that you become conscious of the false effort
you are now making. You become aware of the background; you
perceive how each moment thought is modifying itself through
its own volitional activities born of ignorance and fear. Being
in a state of conflict and at the same time seeking no remedy
or escape, brings about integral thought. This is right effort.
Effortless being is perfection, for in that there is
no self-consciousness.*

Effort, the cause of self-consciousness, is considered necessary for progress, growth, evolution. As long as you make an effort, you think that you are achieving, realizing, coming nearer and nearer truth. But effort is only the awareness of psychological individuality, of separation, of limitation. So effort will not lead you to realize truth.

Effort is the mechanism of the mind attempting to be satisfied. All effort springing from the will to do or not to do must be mechanical, habit-forming, and so cannot bring about rebirth, renewal. Mind ceases to be itself, with this continual effort. Effort exists as long as there is conformity or adjustment to environment.

You make an effort to acquire virtues, pleasures, possessions, to gain greater accumulation and security. If you are not doing this, you go about it negatively by denying these things, and try to develop through effort other subtle self-protections.

Where there is effort based on want, there is choice, which must be based on prejudice, on bias. You are constantly making an effort to achieve, to succeed, to conquer one habit by another, one ideal by another, one longing by another. Effort is utterly futile. It leads to confusion and not to the awakening of intelligence. In the separative process of effort and choice, duality is created, which brings conflict and suffering.

You suffer and you want to escape from that suffering, so you make an effort to seek a remedy, a substitution. But this does not eradicate the cause of suffering. Mind is burdened with many substitutions, many escapes that prevent the birth of choiceless awareness, discernment. Effort creates sorrow and frustration. It is false effort. Right effort is spontaneous discernment of false effort.

Right effort means that you become conscious of the false effort you are now making. You become aware of the background; you perceive how each moment thought is modifying itself through its own volitional activities born of ignorance and fear.

To be in conflict and at the same time to be vibrantly still, neither accepting nor denying it, is not easy. Being in a state of conflict and at the same time seeking no remedy or escape, brings about integral thought. This is right effort. Effortless being is perfection, for in that there is no self-consciousness.

But effort must be made in order to be free of false effort, free of many centuries of tradition, of want, of illusions of fear and fear itself. This effort, consciously made, with the full knowledge of the destructive qualities of fear, of want, of traditional thought and emotion, will set man free of self-consciousness. This is true effort, which leads man to the realization of truth.

CHAPTER 19

Relationship

*Where there is love there is no conflict in relationship. It is only
in a state of resistance that there can be opposites, conflicts. If
you understand this, then you will see that the problem isn't a
question of your resistance in conflict with another, but how this
resistance came into being and how it is to be dissolved.*

To be, is to be related—related to people, ideas and things. Our relationship to people, society, is based on possessiveness and use. Our relationship to things is based on need and greed. Our relationship to ideas is based on opinions, beliefs, creeds, dogmas, ideals.

All relationship is based on egotistic acquisition and possession, effort and control, domination and compulsion, the desire and attempt to gain security.

In relationship you are seeking gratification. So relationship instead of being a progressive action of constant awareness, tends to become a process of self-isolation, limitation. Relationship with others is now based on dependence for your own psychological satisfaction, happiness and well-being. As long as in your relationship with others you are wanting something, there must be conflict. Conflict always arises when there is physiological or psychological dependence.

Life cannot be without relationship, but it is often agonizing because you base it on personal and possessive love. If you can deeply understand this problem of relationship between yourself and another, then perhaps you will understand and solve the problem of your relationship with society. As long as you do not understand individual relationship, you cannot have a peaceful society.

In our personal relationships there is conflict, not only between individuals, but also between the individual and society. Society is the relationship of the individual to the many. Society is the extension, projection of the individual. If the individual does not understand his relationship to the people with whom he is immediately concerned, his actions will produce conflict, personal as well as social. If there is conflict in relationship, there is also the desire to isolate oneself, to withdraw from that relationship that causes pain. This isolation takes the form of either accepting new and pleasanter relationships or withdrawing oneself into a world of ideas. If life is merely a series of events and changing relationships, this will ultimately produce the isolation of the individual. But one cannot withdraw, for all existence is one of relationship. So until one understands and is free of the cause of conflict within oneself, wherever one is, whoever we have relationships with, whatever the circumstances, there must always be conflict. Progressive isolation, which man in conflict longs for, calling it reality, unity, love, detachment and so on, is an escape from reality.

You must understand the basic significance that underlies all strife and conflict in relationship. All strife arises from adjustments between two resistances, two individuals. It is only in a state of resistance that there can be consciousness of relationship, which is but an adjustment between two opposing conflicts. These adjustments between two or more resistances you call relationship. You must see how resistance against each other is created and how that resistance, through accumulation, memories, through experiences is more and more strengthened.

Where there is love there is no conflict in relationship. It is only in a state of resistance that there can be opposites, conflicts. If you understand this, then you will see that the problem isn't a question of your resistance in conflict with another, but how this resistance came into being and how it is to be dissolved.

If the individual does not understand his relationship with another or with society, and the cause of conflict involved in it, then his relationship with another or with society will inevitably lead to friction and antisocial action. Therefore the understanding of relationship becomes very important, the relationship of yourself to possessions, to people, to ideas. And discovering the truth of this lies in understanding yourself in these relationships.

You must take yourself as you are, and this study can be done only in relationship, not in isolation, for to know yourself means to study yourself in action, which is relationship.

In relationship, the primary cause of friction is yourself. If you can only realize that it's not how another acts and reacts that is of primary importance, but how you act and react. If your reaction and action can be fundamentally understood, the relationship will undergo a deep and radical change. In your relationship with another, there is not only the physical problem but also that of thought and feeling on all levels. You can be harmonious with another only when you are harmonious integrally in yourself. It is within yourself that harmony in relationship can be found, not in another, or in environment.

In order to understand yourself it will be necessary for you to go into the question of action and reaction, activity and relationship. You have to understand first what you mean by activity, what you mean by action. Because your whole life is based on activity.

What is the place of activity in relationship? The moment you cease to be active, there is immediately a feeling of nervous apprehension; you feel as though you are not alive, not alert, so you must keep going, keep the activity going. And there is fear of being alone, of going out for a walk alone, of being by yourself, without a book, without a radio, without talking—the fear of sitting quietly without doing something all the time with your hands or with your mind or heart.

In order to escape this unbearable psychological state, you become engrossed in doing things. You are restless, consumed with movement; you do something at any cost, getting on, achieving, trying for success, filling yourself with constant sensation, hoping to achieve a feeling of satisfaction.

So you use relationship with things, ideas and people to feel comfortable, to be gratified, to be something. That is, you use relationship based on thought created by the mind, on ideas, hoping to fulfill your desire, or help you to avoid loneliness, which means that the mind plays an important part in relationship.

As mind is always concerned with protecting itself, with remaining always with the known, it reduces all relationship to the level of habit or of security. Thus relationship becomes merely an activity, a distraction. If you treat relationship as a distraction, as an escape from emptiness, insufficiency, something you do not like, relationship is merely a series of activities involved in relationship.

You now love with the mind; your heart is filled with the things of the mind, sensation. But surely the fabrication of the mind cannot be love. You cannot think about love. You can think about the person whom you love—but that thought is not love, and so, gradually thought takes the place of love. And when the mind directs, there can be no affection. You have filled your heart with the things of the mind and the things of the mind are essentially ideas—what should be and what should not be.

Can relationship be based on an idea? Surely, actions based on an idea must be the continuation of that idea. If you base your relationship on an idea, then such a relationship is merely activity, without comprehension. It is merely carrying out a formula, a pattern, an idea. Because you want something out of relationship, such relationship is always restricting, limiting, confining.

Idea is based on the outcome of a want, of a desire, of a purpose. If I am related to you because I need you, physiologically and psychologically, then that relationship is based on an idea—I want something from you. And such a relationship, based on an idea, cannot be a self-revealing process. It is merely momentum, an activity, in which habit is established. If this is so, is not relationship a self-enclosing activity, which therefore must lead to contention? And if your relationship is based on gratification, then your relationship is bound to create confusion and antagonism. As long as you use relationship as a means of gratification, of escape, as a distraction, it becomes mere thoughtless activity, in which there can be no self-knowledge.

All relationships can be a process of self-revelation. In the process of relationship, you should be aware that you are being revealed to yourself. You are discovering yourself, all the conditions of your being, the ugly and the pleasant. If you are aware, relationship acts as a mirror, reflecting more and more the various states of your thoughts and feelings. If you understand that relationship is a process of self-revelation, then relationship has a very different significance.

But most of you do not want to be revealed in relationship. On the contrary, you use relationship as a means of escaping from and covering up your insufficiency, you own troubles, your own uncertainty. You don't accept relationship as a revealing process, for you are not willing to be shown what you are. If there is conflict or any deep opposition to relationship you try to change it. So relationship, instead of being a progressive action of constant awareness, tends to become a process of self-isolation. The way of desire leads to self-isolation and limitation. But nothing can exist in isolation, and if relationship is merely activity, then relationship has not much significance. If relationship is not a revealing process in which you are discovering yourself, relationship is merely a means of escape from yourself.

Naturally, you question whether it is possible to be related without ideas, without demand, without ownership, possession.

Can there be relationship without the conditioning causes arising from want? Which means, is it possible to relate, to love, without the interference of the mind? Surely that is the problem, is it not? Not only between you and another but between you and society.

If the psychological mind does not interfere, then it is not erecting a barrier, it is not disciplining, suppressing, sublimating itself or the other. Hence what is needed for right relationship is that the mind should not interfere. But this is extremely difficult, because it is not through determination, practice or discipline that the mind ceases to interfere. The mind will cease to interfere only when there is full comprehension of its own process—when there is self-knowledge. Then only is it possible to have right relationship with the one and with the many, free of contention and discord.

To understand this problem, to inquire into it deeply, you have to go into the question of self-knowledge. Because without knowing yourself as you are, without knowing exactly "what is," you cannot have right relationships with another. Do what you will—escape, worship, read, go to the cinema, turn on the radio— as long as there is no understanding of yourself you cannot have right relationships.

If you can fully, completely understand relationship with the one, then perhaps there is a possibility of understanding relationship with the many, with society. For relationship has true significance only when it is a process of self-revelation, when it is revealing to yourself in the very action of relationship, whether it is relationship to things, to people or to ideas. Discernment of the false brings about true action, and true action is not based on an idea, it is immediate, spontaneous, direct, without the process of thought involved. Action from integral thought, without identification or interpretation, awakens creative intelligence, unhindered by fear, by compulsion, by conflict of self-protective choice, by escape, by distraction. Such pure action is the very expression of life, for pure action is born of wisdom and wisdom is action.

In understanding the complexity of relationship, you are creating an understanding that transcends reason and emotion. If you base your relationships merely on reason, on the mind, there is isolation, pride and lack of love. If you base your relationships on emotion, then there is no depth, only sentimentality, which soon evaporates, and no love. The understanding of relationship is impersonal and cannot be destroyed. It is no longer dependent on time.

If we cannot bring forth understanding from the everyday problems of relationship, then to seek such understanding and love in other realms is to live in ignorance and illusion.

Living involves relationship to everything. Man has deemed it his individual prerogative to use relationship, to use all things, in order that he may fulfill his needs and wants, in order to perpetuate himself. In so doing, he has made himself depend upon all things. In the means, his individualized expression, he has created the end, his present state of complete dependence. So man, being dependent, yet of necessity compelled to individual action in order to live, finds himself in constant competition with all other men. It is this process of singly, individually, fulfilling his requirements that has made man acquisitive, exploitive, possessive, greedy. It has made him seek self-gratification in relationship. Such action has divided, separated and isolated him from all men and all things. Man therefore is a living self-contradiction, claiming superiority to all material and living things, proudly acclaiming and upholding his so-called individuality, yet more dependent on material and living things than all other beings. His claims are founded on the development of his individualized consciousness, on achievement and the use he can make of all things. His individual consciousness has separated him from life, denied the unification and rights of all things, and blocked him from living in true relationship. It is through this separative process of thinking-feeling-acting that man has brought upon himself his problems, trouble, chaos and suffering.

Man goes through life meeting each experience in terms of value. He uses the memory of former experiences as guides for present and future action. Experience is used as a means of achieving, acquiring, advancing, succeeding. The very theme of living has become, "What personal advantage can I obtain?" "What do I get out of it?" "What is there in it for me?" Experience used for these ends can only further divide men, set them apart. It is in these divergencies of desire and the attempts to fulfill these ends, that conflict, wars and suffering arise. Our action seeks its fulfillment through forms of attainment, both personal and national. Personalized attainment has given rise to our individualized state of exclusiveness.

CHAPTER 20

Environment

*In deeply discerning the process of fear, there is the awakening
of intelligence, which brings about right conduct. Compulsion
of any kind, whether externally or voluntarily imposed, cannot
awaken intelligence. Imposition is the outcome of fear. Where
there is fear, there cannot be intelligence. When there is freedom
from fear there is no sense of discipline but the spontaneous
adjustment to life.*

Life is eternal, ever becoming. Life is every moment in a state of being born, coming into being. In this coming into being, there is nothing that can be identified as permanent. Life energy is in constant movement, action; each moment of action has never been before and will never be again. But each new moment forms a continuity of movement. Life is ever in a state of perpetual action, flow. Life, the reality that we have been trying to describe, is balance, and this can only be gained by the conflicting forces of nature. Life, the totality, the summation of all life, has no purpose. It is. That life is of no particular temperament or kind; it is neither personal nor impersonal.

All life is energy. This energy manifests in the individual, is conditioned and in turn conditions. Do not attribute to it any divinity or give to it a particular quality. In its self-acting development it creates its own material, the body with its cells and sensation, perception, discrimination, and consciousness. Forms of energy are ever intermingling, and this makes consciousness appear conceptual as well as actual. This energy is abstract as consciousness. The actual is action.

Individual consciousness is the result of ignorance. It is made up of tendencies, wants, cravings. This accumulated ignorance is compounded with energy, which in its self-acting development is unique to individuality. Each individual is unique, different from another. Life is not working to produce a type; life is not creating graven images. Life makes you entirely different, so in diversity must your fulfillment be, not in the production of a type.

Life is not a process of learning, accumulation. Life is not a school in which one passes examinations in learning—in learning from experiences, learning from action, from suffering. Life is to be lived, not learned from. If you regard life as something from which you have to learn, you act superficially. If action, daily living, is but a means toward a reward, a gain, moving toward an end, then action itself has no value. When you have experiences, you say that you must learn from them, understand them. With this attitude, experience itself has no true value for you, because you are looking for a gain through suffering, through action, through experience.

Life is a process of search, a search not for any particular end, but to release creative energy, the creative intelligence in man. It is a process of eternal movement, unhindered by beliefs, by a set of dogmas, or by so-called knowledge. You, through introspection and observation, realize that there is a living reality concealed in matter. At present this realization plays a very little part in your life. But if you unite with life, you unite with everything. How can you unite with life? This can happen by creating that burning desire for truth, which destroys all complications. You ask, "How am I to be in love with life?" Gather experience without wanting to gain by it. "How am I to gather such experience?" Invite it. "How am I to invite it?" Do not seclude yourself from life. Unite with life, for life is conduct, in the manner of your behavior toward another, which is your action. When behavior becomes spontaneous, without desire, then it is unimpeded life in action.

Environment consists of that which is about us, both the actual and the psychological, and that which is in us, both the actual and psychological.

Environment, that which is about us, the outer, consists of people and things—economic, social, religious and political conditions. The psychological environment consists of ideas, their significances and influences.

Our individual environment, consciousness, that which is in us, consists of two forms of the factual and four forms of the psychological. The two forms of factual consciousness, environment, consist of first, the factual elements, which are ours through biological inheritance and ideas derived from them, and second, the factual elements and ideas of outer environment, that which is about us.

The four forms of psychological environment, consciousness, consist of first, our individually formed psychological ideas of the factual elements within us; second, our individually formed psychological ideas of that which is about us, our outer environment; third, the entire content of all psychological ideas, beliefs, ideals that have been acquired from the outside; fourth, our individually formed psychological ideas, which have resulted from our own experiences and from antagonisms to psychological ideas acquired from the outside.

Our vital concern is with environment, not with the conflict, not how to overcome it, not how to run away from it. By questioning the environment both inner and outer, and trying to understand its significance, we shall find out its true worth. Most of us are enmeshed, caught up in the process of trying to overcome, to run away from circumstances, environment. We are not trying to find out what it means—its cause, its significance, its value.

When are you conscious of environment? Only when there is conflict and a resistance to that environment. If you really look at your life, you will see that environment is continually shaping, molding your actions. Out of this, conflict is born.

Conflict can exist only between two false things, between that supposed reality, which you call the "I," which is but the result of environment, and the environment itself. Your mind is concerned with the overcoming of that struggle. In this effort you are perpetuating falseness, and hence creating more conflict and sorrow. But if you understand the significance of environment—wealth, poverty, exploitation, oppression, nationalities, religions, and all the inanities of social life, not trying to overcome them but seeing their significances, then there is the possibility of individual action, a complete revolution of consciousness.

Uncertainty always seeks certainty and accepts the authorized statements of those who offer it. Craving for certainty always creates ignorance and illusion, and it will create psychological instruments of faith and authorities who will reward and punish.

One of the greatest hindrances to the flow of reality is authority. It is one of the most destructive barriers. We have created it in our desire for self-protection and security.

For convenience, let us divide authority into the outer and the inner. The outer authority is environment, habit, tradition, the closed morality of religion, the authority of experts, and the authority of vested interests. The inner authority is the result of our reactions to this compulsion from without. It develops an inner law based on fear, on the self-protective memory of security, and on comfort. It develops also the subtle subjective authority of accumulative memories, prejudices, antipathies, fears, wants, which have become values, ideals, standards. We are continually adjusting and reconciling our conduct to this inner authority. It controls and limits thought and action, and thus creates its own conflict and suffering.

If you deeply examine it, you will see that the mind is constantly accepting or rejecting authority and conditioning itself by new values and standards born of craving for self-protection. Authority is the same whether objective or subjective. Authority implies shaping, imitation, a control, a conditioning, whether imposed externally or by inward effort and exertion. Authority is the process of imitation. It makes man into an imitative machine, into a cog whether in a social or religious machine.

You can find out how to live intelligently only when you understand environment, not only the objective but the subjective, which is infinitely subtle. You must individually come into conflict with it. It is only in conflict, in suffering, that you, the individual, begin to discern the true significance of environment. As most people are afraid of coming into contact with suffering, they would rather perceive the significance of environment only intellectually. They leave the responsibility of action to the mass, a vague and unreal entity, which they hope will miraculously alter their environment and so bring them happiness.

To understand the cause of authority, you must follow the mental and emotional process that creates it. First of all you feel empty, and in order to get rid of that feeling, you make an effort; by that effort you create opposites; you create a duality, which but increases the incompleteness and emptiness. You do not understand that you are responsible for such authorities as religion, politics, morality, and such authorities as social and economic standards.

As you come to understand external standards; you will want to liberate yourself from them and to develop your own inner standard. This inner standard that you call "spiritual reality" only creates another division, another duality.

You need to understand that you are compelled into action by both outer and inner compulsions. Outward compulsion, the restraint of environment upon the individual, crushes the individual into the steel frame of standards of morality, of religious ideas, of moral edicts, of economic competitiveness, exploitation, possessiveness, of political domination, control, regimentation, of social restrictions, demands, conventions. As the individual is crushed from the outside he seeks an escape into a world which he calls the inner. He builds up a romantic haven of escape in which he seeks compensation for the loss and suffering in the outer world. He then creates the inner world, begins to develop an inner law and creates his own individual restraints, compulsion. This he calls self-discipline, which he then calls the higher self. Both inner and outer compulsions are controlling, compelling.

Any conduct born of compulsion, whether it be the compulsion of reward or punishment, of gain or loss, of good or bad, of right or wrong, of fear or love, is not right conduct. It is merely an imitation, a forcing and training of the mind according to certain ideas, in order to avoid conflict. This kind of discipline, imposed or voluntary, does not lead to right conduct. Right conduct is possible only when you understand the full significance of the self-activating process of ignorance.

In deeply discerning the process of fear, there is the awakening of intelligence, which brings about right conduct. Compulsion of any kind, whether externally or voluntarily imposed, cannot awaken intelligence. Imposition is the outcome of fear. Where there is fear, there cannot be intelligence. Where intelligence is functioning there is spontaneous adjustment without the process of discipline. So the question is not whether discipline is right or wrong, or whether it is necessary, but how the mind can be free from self-created fear. When there is freedom from fear there is no sense of discipline but the spontaneous adjustment to life.

We have built up through the centuries an environment, both outer and inner, of such illusion as authority, imitativeness, beliefs, ideals, opinions. We have developed a consciousness, which maintains and demands individualized action. This consciousness keeps man in conflict with his environment, with ideas, things and people.

The difficulty is that our thinking is conditioned thinking. We are either French or English or German or Hindu with our particular religious, political, social, educational and economic backgrounds, through its screen of conditioning, this psychological environment, we try to meet the problems of life, and thereby increase our problems. We do not meet life without conditioning; we meet it with a particular training, with a particular background, experience.

Being conditioned we meet life according to our particular patterns, with our particular beliefs, ideas, ideals, knowledge and processes of living. This reaction only creates more problems.

Obviously then, we have to understand and remove these conditionings, which increase our problems. Most of us are unaware that we are conditioned. Our conditioning is the result of our background and our desire for security. After all, the society about us is the outcome of our desire to be secure, to be safe, to be permanent in our own particular form of conditioning. Being unaware of our conditioning, we continue to create more problems. We have so many beliefs to which we cling, and these backgrounds, these conditionings, prevent us from actually meeting life as it is. We are always meeting life with our inadequate responses, and so never understand life except through our particular conditionings. The challenge of life is in constant transformation, is in constant flux. We have to understand not the challenge, but our reaction to it. Our concern must be with this environment, not with the conflict, not how to overcome it, not how to run away from it.

Man recognizes a living reality in matter. He mistakenly considers this life energy to be manifested in himself as individual consciousness. He considers that his consciousness is the very essence of reality. He does not recognize that his present consciousness is the formulated result of self-protective and self-perpetuating action; the result of craving, wanting and other innumerable tendencies; that it is the composite of continuous desire, the product of fear, operates through and in himself, perpetuates itself through a self-developed mechanism and that this self-developed mechanism and consciousness are actually one and the same. Consciousness is the functional evidence of energy in the abstract, the body being materialized energy in the actual. That consciousness is this energy, and this energy is used to perpetuate consciousness.

It is through constant contact and resistance to environment, both the outer and the inner, that we have developed the present form of consciousness. It is the result of conflict. Through this consciousness, this conflict, we have evaluated and judged all things. We have chosen to be, possess, use and attain those things that best fulfill our self-perpetuating purpose. This type of action has given rise to our ideals, beliefs, dogmas, creeds, standards and systems of living. These form our consciousness.

CHAPTER 21

Memory and Time

*When you meet an experience fully, completely, without
bias or prejudice, it leaves no scar of psychological memory.
The factual components of memory will remain, but the
psychological thought–feeling reactions will be absent; there will
be no carryover, no continuance of psychological substance or
motivation for future use. No psychological memory
of that experience will remain to direct, control, limit and take
over action.*

Memory is the total residuum of factual and psychological experience of both the actual and the false. Psychological memory consists of the interpretations, motivations and the manner in which the psychological elements of experiences are used.

Psychological memory is the many layers of self-protective responses against life. Self-consciousness is the consciousness of the particular, the "I," the individuality. Memory is the perpetuation of the "I" consciousness. Man will always have memory, factual memory, but it is not necessary for him to have, live through and fulfill life with psychological memory. Psychological memory is the falsely created and illusory use of memory. It is self-made, consisting only of man's impressions and interpretations, his psychological ideas and feeling reactions, which are not real, though they may seem so to him. They exist only as long as he sustains them, as long as he supports, uses and creates more of them. In each experience, there is the factual and the psychological. The factual memory consists of what is, the psychological memory consists of your self-interpreted significances—how your conditioned thinking and feeling reactions interpret your experiences and how they should be considered and used. This psychological process can be ended. It is self-sustained and will die if not kept alive. Psychological memory consists of experience, incident, fear, hope, longing, belief, idea, interpretation, perception, opinion, conclusion, concept, prejudice, tradition, action, deed, with all their subtle and complex reactions.

We are concerned with these psychological memories and the cessation of their function. It is the understanding of their significances and the liberation from them that is our concern.

There are various kinds of psychological memory. One kind of memory is concerned with beliefs, principles, ideals. All ideals and principles are really dead things of the past. The memory of ideals persists when you cannot meet or understand the full movement of life. Then there is the memory, pleasant or unpleasant, which precipitates itself in the mind, even though you do not want it. Uninvited past incidents come into your mind because you are not vitally interested in the present, because you are not fully alive in the present.

There is another kind of memory, that of recollection. When you experience a beautiful incident, and later, when you are, say, at your daily routine work, your mind returns to that scene. Why? Because when you are involved in what is not pleasant, your mind tends automatically to return to the pleasant experience of yesterday. You dwell in memory, to make the present tolerable. Therefore the past lingers in the present.

There is the memory of self-discipline, which is will. Will is also memory. You discipline yourself through the pattern of memory.

Psychological memory is born, created from incompleteness of action. When you have an experience that you cannot fully understand, if you do not understand an incident, if you do not live completely in an experience, the memory of that incident, experience, lingers in your mind. It remains there to be used for a self-protective purpose and action and returns to your mind in experiences that follow. You are constantly acting through this veil of memories, and therefore your action is always incomplete.

An experience that has been understood no longer remains in the memory, so action does not return to it for further use. But as you do not live in action, but in constant self-protective reaction, psychological memory is always there and is used to determine your response in experience.

You need to realize that psychological memory is an impediment to intelligence; that memory is independent of intelligence. Memory acts on and through its own substance without the direction of intelligence. And in so doing, acts as a resistance against life, against intelligence.

Psychological memory creates barriers and leaves barriers behind. Memory guides us through experiences; it is a form of self-discipline, a perpetuation of the "I." Psychological memory thwarts, stupefies and makes the ever-becoming intelligence impossible. Psychological memory is a barrier to right action.

The content and nature of psychological memory is man's limited interpretation of experiences. These memories and these alone interpret all new experiences. By them you will judge the new. Your action will always be one of self-protective interpretation. There will be bias and prejudice against all that does not agree with your experiences, your values, your beliefs.

Because you are constantly acting through psychological memory, you have never a day, never a moment, of rich full completeness. These memories are always impeding, curtailing, limiting your actions.

Since you have many layers of memories arising from incomplete actions, there comes into being that self-consciousness, which you call the ego and which is but a series of memories, an illusion without reality, without substance.

As long as there is the scar of psychological memory, there must be the division of time as past, present and future. As long as mind believes in the idea that action must be divided into past, present and future, there is identification through time and therefore continuity. From this arises the fear of death, the fear of loss of love.

When you become aware of these memories, these barriers, when you become aware with your heart and mind in the midst of a crisis, that very awareness frees your mind. Without effort that very awareness frees your mind. Without effort the barriers that have prevented your complete action disappear.

When you meet an experience fully, completely, without bias or prejudice, it leaves no scar of psychological memory. The factual components of memory will remain, but the psychological thought-feeling reactions will be absent; there will be no carryover, no continuance of psychological substance or motivation for future use. No psychological memory of that experience will remain to direct, control, limit and take over action.

Self-consciousness, or that consciousness of the particular, the "I," the individuality, is a bundle of memories. Time is the field in which it can function. Time—that is, psychological time—is psychological memory or self-consciousness. Psychological time is the continuous past, present and future. Psychological time is an illusion; it is but the incompleteness of action. Chronological time is the present, is the now. Memory, which is the psychological time of the past, uses the present to project the past into the future. Psychological time is the result of those volitional activities of craving, which bind and give a sense of continuity to life. Chronological time is ever in a state of being born, a state that has never been nor ever will be again. It is ever new, ever in movement.

Psychological time on the other hand, is the utilization of past, present and future. As psychological memory, it does not give discernment of experiences; it makes you only more clever, more cunning, when meeting or avoiding experiences.

The idea of time as a process of unfolding is the cultivated method of postponement. You do not meet now the thing that confronts you because you are afraid; you do not want to meet experience wholly, either because of your prejudice or because of the desire to postpone.

As long as there is the scar of psychological memory, there must be the division of time as past, present and future. As long as mind is tethered to the idea that action must be divided into the past, present and future, there is identification of me and mine through time and therefore a continuity from which arises the fear of death, the fear of loss of love. Psychological time is the habit of the mind.

Only when the mind is free of this division of time can true action result. If you perceive and live completely in the very thing you are experiencing, the mind frees itself from the idea of progressive time.

CHAPTER 22

Self-Knowledge

*The understanding of oneself and others is not fulfilled by
gathering knowledge about the function of the psychological
mind, but is an understanding that comes of its own, outside
the domain of the intellect. And to discover what is beyond
thought, beyond the intellect, beyond memory, psychological
thought and feeling must come to an end.*

You who are studying what you consider to be fulfillment through self-knowledge, will find that you develop an unexpected and intensely disturbing accentuation of self-consciousness; an intensification of the "me," the very thing you are trying to free yourself from. Through self-exploration you become more and more concerned with and about yourself. There is increasing concern with and about things, ideas, people and the critical judgment of your relationship to them. Regardless of what measures you use, self-consciousness increases and you become more firmly and deeply caught in it. In this psychological state of mind you have become critical of yourself, but more critical of others. You place undue emphasis on what you consider to be faulty ideas and behavior of others and judge them more frequently and severely than yourself. This is of primary significance, for your behavior portrays the attempt to escape from self-consciousness.

When you are caught in self-consciousness, you become aware of more inner conflicts in your life than ever before. Sometimes you mistake this increased inner turmoil, conflict, to be awakening and discernment, but it is only intensified psychological moralization. Often you are filled with a sense of utter futility and frustration. You feel helpless, blocked and trapped.

But this does not prevent you from trying to give the impression that you have great knowledge. Instead of realizing the significance of your psychological state of mind, you alternate between judgment of yourself and others, and your life becomes a battlefield of conflicting concepts and emotional irrationalities. In your blindness, you become the wielder of a club, both upon yourself and others.

You do not realize that you have mistaken an intensified "I," an increased "me," for spontaneous alertness, sensitivity and

188

understanding. Instead of freeing yourself from the problems of self-achievement, you have magnified all elements of the self. In your mind, little things have become big, are evaluated out of all proportion to their significance. Everything has become distorted and distended, and the nonessential has become monstrously essential. You are the center and creator of self-expansion.

Why have you intensified the "I"? Where does the error lie in the search for self-knowledge? You find the answer in the fact that there is self-consciousness the moment you desire to gain something through self-knowledge. Self-consciousness arises only when there is the desire for achievement. This is the key to the problem. You are using self-knowledge to get what you want. It is important to understand that you may, in attempting self-knowledge, be unconscious of hidden self-motivations. You must realize it indicates that you are using knowledge for the "self," not self-knowledge, to fulfill an unknown objective or objectives.

Your means of achievement and protection is expressed in many ways—but each way has but a single objective, the attainment and achievement of psychological desire. For example, you are using knowledge about the self for assurance and security of position.

You have distant objectives, to find truth, reality, wisdom; or you want to assure yourself of perpetuation and immortality; or you want to get rid of what you consider to be bad traits, characteristics and become virtuous, honorable. In your immediate relationships you have self-fulfilling desires and objectives to have dominance, power and control over things and people. You want to feel superior, more important. You use your daily contact with another competitively to show that you know more than the other, or to belittle the other. You use knowledge of the self to point out what you consider to be false in others, thereby gaining delight in your astuteness. Or you use it to augment or restore vanity, pride or other qualities. But most significant of all, you use this knowledge to avoid facing up to that which is in yourself, to avoid recognition, acknowledgment and acceptance of the false elements in yourself. Self-achievement is the hidden purpose. You have achieved complete escape from that which is in yourself; you have used the ultimate in self-deception, knowledge about the self, not self-knowledge. Unconsciously, whether known to you or not, you have been pursuing self-knowledge in the same manner and with the same means you use when seeking the fulfillment of any other personal desires or objectives.

Why was it possible for you to make this mistake in your approach to self-knowledge? It was practically impossible for it to be otherwise, for in the beginning you come seeking, you come as a self-achieving moral process, in which your habitual manner of meeting and handling the problems of life is one of expectant gain for yourself.

When you contacted the "new process of transformation," encountered new experiences and aspects about life and yourself, you reacted self-protectively in one of three ways. These three forms of reaction are the basic foundation of your self-protective psychological thinking-feeling processes. You have been unconsciously using them since the beginning of your conditioning, and they are the criteria of your responses in all your experiences.

In contacting the "new," the unknown, your response to it is in reaction. Either you avoid or ignore the "new," the unknown; or, with varying degrees of effort, appropriate that which you want of it and convert or transpose it into that which you are, the "old," your psychologically conditioned state; or, you accept it without reservation as a new form of belief, or a new way of life.

190

Your acceptance of the new follows one of two procedures. The one in which you interpret that which you hear, read or experience in terms of that which you are, the old ideas and beliefs, using the new merely to confirm and support, whenever possible, that which you consider to be "right." Then there is the other procedure in which you believe you totally accept the new and become these ideas in consciousness. But in fact you do not. You become your individual psychological interpretation of them. Then you use these new ideas self-protectively. You act on and through your interpretation of their significances, in order to destroy that which you now are, the old, your former ideas and beliefs in which you have been conditioned. Hence your motivation and activity remains the same, a self-achieving process. Whether you follow the first or second procedure, the psychological condition that results is the same, namely, an expanded and intensified "I," with increased inner conflict. In the use of these self-achieving processes you completely trap yourself, for you are trying to use one part of the mind to change or get rid of another part of the mind. And can mind, using mind, get rid of mind? Obviously not. The mind can only add to mind when using the new to approve or deny that which is old.

Hence, through unconscious desire for self-achievement by means of self-knowledge you find yourself in ever increasing psycho-emotional self-consciousness and frustration. You do not realize that these interpretations at best could be nothing more than self-interpretations. You did not know that you live a life of constant achievement, attainment and possession in all that you do, and in all that you contact, attain and possess, whether it be things, ideas or people, and in this case, "knowledge about the self." You use your conditioned thinking-feeling processes to establish within a constant sense of confirmation, satisfaction and security. Also, as you come to the "new" with an intellectually blind self-protective process, you cannot understand that which is being presented. It was inevitable from the beginning that there would be engendered self-deception, confusion and self-consciousness.

As you did not know another state of consciousness was necessary, or even possible, it was inevitable that you would come to the search for self-knowledge expecting to get something out of it for yourself. So likewise, as your present process of living is totally self-protective, for you possess no other, nor did you know of another, or the necessity for it, you came as you are, a self-achieving psychological process, whose primary intent is the fulfillment of your desire. You have attempted self-knowledge with the only means you had at your command.

Finding your endeavors fruitless, empty, without reward or gain, you begin to question. Is it possible to free oneself from this untenable situation? Is it the result of not having sufficient knowledge? Is it possible to go beyond?

If you consider your situation to be the result of insufficient knowledge, you will seek an authority, a new religion or nonreligion, hoping through them you can obtain a solution to the problem. From this procedure you become further removed from the problem or the solution of the problem. It is only in the technical sphere, the factual physical, that the intellectual procedure is applicable, in which another can help us.

Intellectual thought, whether applied by yourself or another, is incapable of solving your psychological problems. There are two reasons for this. First, thought can only discover its own projections, that which it can conceive. Second, it cannot discover anything new. Thought can only recognize that which it has experienced. Psychological thought is man's own creation; he can only recognize those things of his own making. Intellectual thought can and does investigate the thoughts, feelings and behavior of man, the complexities of his nature, the problems which he has created, and makes determinations through observation, reason and instrumentation. But all these conclusions are in the field of thought, the field of effects, not cause. The intellect, cannot solve psychological problems, for the mind of man is also psychological, superficial in its entirety, and all that can come from it is more of the same thing. Blindness cannot correct blindness. The falsely created psychological process of thinking cannot correct the false elements in it.

When the intellect is used to solve psychological problems, it can only make adjustments within the field of the intellectual process. This procedure gives only temporary aid of an artificial nature. It is an adjustment in illusion, the mending of one falsity by another, but never a complete release from the problem. Through psychological thought man can only perceive projections of his own making, not causes. In this manner he may know something about the problem, but not the solution of the problem. Mind knowing about its interpretations, its handiwork, must come to recognize that all it finds out will only be psychological ideas and knowledge about his or the others' psychological self. It will not be the actual. As the intellect cannot be used to understand something which is not in the field of the intellect, but beyond it, all that can be obtained are inductive and deductive conclusions. In using the intellect we simply deal with the mechanics of the mind. Our psychological thinking processes are nothing more than an automatic mechanical process, whose problems when solved by the intellect are nothing more than an adjustment, a substitution or a replacement of psychological parts, applied to the psychological machine.

The intellectual subjective consciousness considers individual psychological problems to be different and believes it solves each individual problem differently with adequate psychological remedies. This conceived difference, both in the problems and in the psychological remedies used, is not a difference in kind, but only in degree. The psychological means that creates the problem may vary, but the psycho-emotional dualistic process of thinking and feeling in handling the problem is always the same, a psychological self-protective, self-seeking activity, mechanical in nature, artificial in context, made by man. Hence both the thoughts and emotions of the individual, the problem, and those of an authority, the psychologist, the remedy, are only variations of the same psychological process. Hence modern psychology, because the individual and the psychologist are machines, habitual processes, who fulfill their psychological processes essentially in the same way, can only give temporary aid and this in the level of psychological thought, which arises out of manmade individual interpretations of his impressions. To these interpretations he will give different labels, administer them to another, thinking he has determined the cause when it will be only an effect, a result, whose corrective significance is negligible. Like all mechanical things when repaired, the mind will operate for a time, then it will fail again and will have to be readjusted and stabilized. When the mind thinks it is applying therapeutic psychology to human affairs, it is simply applying mental mechanics, not freeing man from his false means of thinking, feeling and acting.

The solution to man's psychological problems lies outside the scope of the intellect. Their solution requires a different approach, procedure and a different attitude of mind and consciousness; one that is free of psychological thought and emotion. The understanding of oneself and others is not fulfilled by gathering knowledge about the function of the psychological mind, but is an understanding that comes of its own, outside the domain of the intellect. And to discover what is beyond thought, beyond the intellect, beyond memory, psychological thought and feeling must come to an end. Psychological problems can be understood only through passive awareness, an integrated state of the three forms of consciousness, which form the common presence of man, and not through one's intellect or the intellect of another. For this fulfillment to be, we alone must do it, for no other can do it for us.

CHAPTER 23

Security

When you discover, not theoretically but actually, when you directly experience attachment to a belief, to a particular idea or formula, then you will see that there comes a freedom from that particular form of security. And in that state of uncertainty, which is not isolation, which is not fear, there is creative being. Uncertainty is essential for creative being.

Man is constantly seeking his own security, that which he calls happiness. His primary interest and activity is in the pursuit of those things that afford him the greatest sense of satisfaction and assurance. His whole movement in life is in his own behalf, that he may obtain those things he thinks necessary for his self-fulfillment. His way is narrow, discriminatory, selfish.

He can never be secure, but he thinks he can. He also thinks his forms of security are real and right not only for himself but also for others. And because of this type of thinking, he tries to force others to think and do as he does. To him, his way of living takes precedence over all else. His way is best.

But security has to do with externals, destructibles—a matter of resources, boundary lines, governments of methods, money, property, possessions, position, place and the success in fulfilling them. Security has to do with things that are impermanent, ideas that are changeable and people who are unpredictable. In these there is no security.

Regardless of the fact that man can never be secure, all his efforts are given to achieve it. He is in constant reaction to all changing circumstances and conditions that may interfere or disrupt his various attempts at self-fulfillment. His whole activity is concentrated on this static and false purpose. It is because of this constant pursuit of security that man keeps not only himself, but all others in a state of agitation, contention, conflict and suffering. Such is the behavior of man.

This kind of living and behavior arises from the unconscious level of his mind. That is how man is functioning, from the acquired and instinctive processes of living.

In lower forms of life there is always a rivalry going on for existence, for subsistence, for fulfillment. On this level, constant strife exists. It is their way of life. They are contending with all externals to maintain their integrity in order that they may fulfill life's use and purpose. They do not seek security, they live in the moment, instinctively doing that which is necessary to their being. All things are in a state of contention. They are either in a formative state, the constructive phase of living; or in the deteriorating state— returning to primary substance. Even though all forms of life are individually and often collectively in contention with each other for existence, if we look more deeply behind these contentions, we will see that all things, life as a totality supports and maintains itself, even though the individual manifestation gives up body and life, its total substance. The law of the life force is function and use, and in turn, to use and be used by life. All forms of life become the means whereby other forms of life live and function. In this there is no selfish individual fulfillment. The different forms and expressions of life are being used by life, for life's purposes. Life is constantly functioning; there is perpetual change. All creation gives evidence that function predicates an aim, a purpose. The only way these creations fulfill life's purpose is by functioning according to their nature. So life's purpose, manifested in man, is not the search for security. That would be like life being made secure from life. The life force wants to use itself, including you, in its own way—in its own manner, to fulfill its purpose; it is a method, a means by which all things, including you, are but a means to fulfill itself. All forms of life are the result of life operating on itself through experiences with itself. Hence all forms of life have a developed functional purpose to life. Basic functioning is always a channel for the expression of life and its purpose; a creation of life, by life, for the flow through of life. Thus for man, his perpetual search for external or internal security is false. The search for individual happiness is the false use of consciousness.

So you see that the first illusion in which you are caught is desire for assurance, the desire for both outer, physical, and inner, psychological, security. Each individual is constantly seeking and attempting to create security for himself, both objectively and subjectively, and therefore his reaction to life is one of continual self-defense. This process perpetuates ignorance, which prevents the mind from acting fully, completely. It develops its own particularity, which we call individuality, which inevitably must come into conflict with the many other individualities. This is the fundamental cause of conflict and suffering.

There is so-called physical security through things that are acquired, for the most part selfishly. Some of you are seeking security through wealth, comfort and the power over others that wealth gives you. You are interested in social differences and social privileges that give you a preferred position from which you derive satisfaction. The longing for physical security shows itself in the desire to have a substantial bank account, a good position and the desire to be considered somebody in town and in the striving for degrees and titles. The objective search for security through egotistic power is essentially based on fear and so on exploitation. If you look at the present system, you will see that it is a series of cunning forms of exploitation of man by man. Family, class, nation become the very center of exploitation.

Through accumulation you hope to have the assurance of certainty; certainty that takes away all doubt and anxiety; certainty that gives you surety of choice. You want to be certain, you avoid uncertainty; you want to be certain in your affection, you want to be certain in your knowledge, you want to be certain in your experiences, because that certainty gives you a sense of assurance, a sense of well-being in which there is no disturbance, no shock of experience, the shock of a new quality of being. Your whole life is based on this desire for security, certainty.

Physical security is a crude form of security. Some of you become dissatisfied with physical security and turn to security of a more subtle form, which you call "spiritual." There is no real difference between the two. You establish and vitalize those things which you call religion and organized beliefs. You establish a system of philosophical thought in which you are caught, to which you become a slave. To be subjectively certain, you seek what you call immortality. You accept teachers who promise this immortality, and you come to regard them as authorities, to be worshipped, to be feared. And when there is this fear, there must be dogmas, creeds, beliefs, ideals and traditions.

What you call religion is an organized form of individual self-protection, for subjective inward security. To administer this authority based on fear, there must be priests who become your exploiters. You are the creators of your own exploitation. Religion has become an organized belief, a crystallized form of thought, morality, of oppression, domination. Religion is a subjective submission to a system that you hope will assure you security.

Though you may not have any religious belief, yet you have the desire to be subjectively, inwardly secure, so in this sense you also have the religious spirit. There is mental security found in ideas, beliefs, in the pursuit of virtues, systems, certainties, and so-called knowledge. There is also security through "service to others." You like to lose yourself in the bog of activity, in work. You find great satisfaction in accumulated knowledge, experience, in your capacity to do things with your hands or with your mind. In that capacity you seek certainty because in that state, the mind need never be disturbed, there is no anxiety, no fear, no new experience.

Through this activity, this hope for security and certainty, you seek to escape from facing your own incessant struggle.

Security is an escape. And since most people are trying to escape, they have made themselves into machines of habit in order to avoid conflict. They create religions, beliefs, ideas; they worship the image they call God; they try to forget their inability to face the struggle by losing themselves in work. All these are ways of escape.

The mind, seeking inward certainty, through property, work, through people, through ideas, does not desire to be disturbed and be made uncertain. Have you not often noticed how the mind rebels against anything new—a new idea, a new experience, a new state? When it does experience a new state, the mind immediately brings it into the field of itself, into the field of the known. The mind is always functioning within the field of certainty, within the field of security, therefore it can never experience something beyond itself.

Thus, in seeking your own security, certainty, you have created many impediments of which you are entirely unconscious. These impediments are turning you into a machine, they are preventing you from being a true individual.

One of our great difficulties is that in trying to find security, not only in the economic world, but also in the psychological or so-called spiritual world, we destroy physical security. Physical security is made impossible by the desire, by the anxiety, by the psychological necessity of seeking inward security. In the search for economic and psychological, spiritual security, we create certain ideas, we cling to certain beliefs. Through their use we hope to create inward security. By these means we invariably sacrifice and destroy outward physical security. It is this desire for inward security that divides and destroys relationship, separating us each from the other. Our problem is not to seek a formula or system that will bring about outward security, but to find out why the mind is constantly seeking psychological security. Our search for outer, physical security arises from our inner psychological insecurity. It is only when there is freedom from all desire to be inwardly secure that there is a possibility for outer security, for all humanity to have the physical things that are necessary for survival.

Security, self-protection, whether spiritual, economic, political or social, is the outcome of insufficiency, in which there is no intelligence, in which there is no creative thinking, in which there is a constant battle between the "you" and society.

Each must realize that this continual search for happiness, for truth, for reality, for health, this constant desiring is cultivated by each one of us in order to be certain, to be secure.

If you become conscious of your thoughts you will discern that they have their roots in fear. They are the outcome of the desire on the part of the individual to be secure. For the man who is truly uncertain there is hope; but for the man who is entrenched in belief, or in what he calls intuition, there is very little hope; for he has closed the door of uncertainty, doubt, and takes rest and consolation in security.

Obviously then, what is important is for each one to find out where he is attached, in what he is seeking security; and if he is really interested, he can discover in what manner, through what experience, through what belief, the mind is seeking security, certainty.

If you become conscious of these limitations, conflict arises. But you do not want conflict. You desire satisfaction, security and so these hindrances continue to create turmoil. It is this very desire for certainty that prevents you from inquiring into the need for freedom from inward security.

You will find true happiness, reality, fulfillment only when you come into conflict with these values that now oppress and limit your mind. Merely examining these values intellectually does not reveal their true significance. Intellectual examination will not create conflict, and it is only through suffering that you begin to understand the deep concealed meaning in false values. When you discover, not theoretically but actually, when you directly experience attachment to a belief, to a particular idea or formula, then you will see that there comes a freedom from that particular form of security. And in that state of uncertainty, which is not isolation, which is not fear, there is creative being. Uncertainty is essential for creative being.

CHAPTER 24

Fear

As fear cannot allow you to be yourself, how then are you to overcome all fear? How are you to free yourself from all fear whether conscious or unconscious? If you are unconscious of fear, become conscious of it. Become aware of your thoughts and actions and soon you will be conscious of fear. You must be aware of the whole process of the will, of its struggles, its escapes, its miseries.

Fear is both inborn and acquired, psychological. It is related to the past and manifests in the present.

Inborn fear has been one of the means, one of the forms of energy, that has aided life in nature to develop and become focused in the individual. It has the needed capacity, range, intensity and force to aid, protect and help perpetuate life in man. Inborn fear is of a different quality from acquired fear. Inborn fear is direct, forceful, alerting, informative and is present only in possible or actual danger. It is not born of pleasure and is not the product of psychological desire. Its purpose is to give guidance and help to preserve and perpetuate life. Inborn fear is natural, real and necessary.

Acquired or psychological fear is manmade fear, which has within it the range, intensity and force of psychological desire, for it is the product of desire. Acquired fear is not concerned with self-preservation; it is concerned with acquisition. Acquired fear functions exactly opposite to inborn fear, for it is destructive, blinding, confusing and misleading. Its range of function varies from subtle, cunning pleasure seeking, to raging, paralyzing intensities. Acquired fear is always present in psychological experience. It leaves a scar of memory, which never goes away. Psychological, acquired fear is illusory, unnatural, and not necessary for either unconscious or conscious life. It retards and destroys both forms of life.

Our concern is with this falsely created, conditionally acquired, psychological fear, in its formation, in its present use in our living, how it comes about, the falsity of its function and the liberation from it.

What forms of fear are there? Of what are we afraid?

Psychological fear will exist in different forms, grossly and subtly as long as there is the self-active process of ignorance engendered by the activities of want. There are various forms of fear—fear of the future, of death, of responsibility, etc. Most people in the world—it does not matter who they are—are bound by fear of being "wrong"; fear of heaven and hell, fear of approval or disapproval. They are afraid of innumerable things, of convention, of what others might say—all the time they are fearing. Most people are afraid of conditions that they have not tested, fear of the unknown. There is the fear of ill health, fear of the weather, fear of losing, fear of poverty, fear of not getting, and so forth. One is afraid of a possible accident, or of people, or of some personal relationship and so on. In some cases it is the outward situations of life that are making us afraid, and if we free ourselves from them we think that we will be free of fear. But that is not so. For example, can you free yourself from other people? You may be able to escape from a particular person, but wherever you are, you are always in relation to someone. You may be able to create an illusion into which you can withdraw, build a wall between your neighbor and yourself, and thereby feel protected. You may separate yourself through social division, through virtues, beliefs, acquisitions, and so free yourself from your neighbor. But this is not freedom from fear, this is the use of fear to escape another form of fear.

Fear is in your heart when you are attached. The mind has gathered certain values, treasures, and it intends to guard them. If the worth of these possessions is questioned, there is the awakening of fear. If you have anything in your heart that you are guarding, secrets, hidden motives, guilt, fancied or real, there is fear. You are bound to create walls against fear, and this resistance is called by many names: love, virtue, character, will, justified right, etc.

Have you anything that may be taken away from you, your position, your ambition, desires, hope, love, your life? Where there is attachment, there is fear. Unless you know what you are holding on to, fear must continue, though you may desire to get rid of it. Freedom from fear is not the reward of nonattachment. Detachment is really a form of protection—a fulfillment in fear—against suffering, against unfulfilled want or desire.

Fear comes when you have a dark corner in your mind or in your heart, in which you keep unsolved problems. It is the phantom that follows every human being as a shadow, for it is fear that binds, that warps, that perverts; it is fear that suffocates every human being. And your immediate reaction when afraid is to strengthen those walls of resistance, strengthen them so as to be secure. You know fear when your resistance is broken, weakened; when the walls of your self-protection have been broken into, then you are conscious of fear.

But there must be fear so long as there is the "I" process, the consciousness of want, which limits action. All action born of want creates further limitation. As long as there is this limited consciousness called the "I" there must be fear. This constant presence of wanting, with its many activities, does not free mind from fear; it gives the "I" process an identity and continuity. Action springing from want will always create fear and hinder intelligence and the spontaneous adjustment to life. But you want to be secure, both here and in the hereafter. The desire for security creates fear, and being afraid, you try to escape through the illusion of religion, deals, sensation and activity. As long as there is fear, which is born of self-protective desires, mind will be caught in the net of illusions. If you look at it, you will see that fear exists so long as this idea of self-preservation continues, so long as the mind clings to self-consciousness, egotism. Egotism is so subtle, it expresses itself in so many ways, that you are often totally unconscious of it. It expresses itself through the search for security. Through all these attempts at accumulation, protection, you hope to have assurance of certainty. Thus in the search for security, there is born the fear of not gaining and the fear of loss. Where there is fear, conscious or unconscious, intelligent understanding of life becomes impossible. Fear can only breed fear and so ignorance continues.

Desire is the cause, the seed of fear, this craving to become, to be, to achieve.

Any dependence on things, ideas or on people breeds fear. When you rely psychologically on a person, on a leader, or on a group for your understanding, for your security, for your hope or love; when you rely on things or ideas for your certainty, for your fulfillment, what takes place? Does it not create fear? Or being afraid, do you not depend on others for assurance?

The self is the root of all fear—the will to be satisfied, the will to survive, the will to continue—this is the very root of all fear. The psychological mind is the instrument developed for the survival of "I," for self-protection, for resistance, and therefore it is an instrument of fear. From desire springs reason, conclusion, action whose values and moralities are based on the will to survive, to be satisfied, to be certain. The mind breaks itself up into all dualities, and so is engendering its own fear.

The whole of life is based on pursuit of individual security, safety, and comfort. In this search for security, naturally fear is born. When the mind is trying to evade struggle, conflict, sorrow, when you are seeking comfort, you create various avenues of escape, and these avenues of escape become your illusions.

In order to escape fear, you create faith. It is fear that creates faith in man. You say, "If I get rid of faith, then I shall be left with fear, and so have gained nothing." So you prefer to live in illusion, clinging to your fantasies.

When there is fear, then religions and authorities, which you have created in your search for security, offer you the opiate you call faith or love of God. Thus you merely cover up fear. You reject old faiths and accept new ones; but the real cause, the root of fear, is never solved.

You never go to a temple with your solved problems. You go to a church or temple to worship or to pray, when there is a problem confronting you to which you cannot find a solution, when there is a situation of which you are fearful. That is what religions have become a peg on which to hang all your unsolved problems and fears.

Through possessive love, ego exaltation, egotism is developed and maintained to cover over the poverty of being, to escape from emptiness, loneliness. Through acquisitiveness and possessiveness of things you try to escape from the uncertainties of life. For most people, desire becomes merely an escape, a flight from actuality. Desire is the psychological mechanism of escape, of habit formation. It creates the values upon which your whole life is based.

What are these values of habit based on? If you discern deeply, you will see that these values and ideas, these phantoms of the past, are based on fear, which is the outcome of individual search for security. In essence, these restraints, which are your values and guides, which you call the outer and the inner values, are born of want and so there is fear, compulsion, influence and the desire for power. Compulsion is the outward expression of fear. Where there is fear there cannot be intelligence. As long as you have not understood that there will be this division in life as the outer and the inner. Therefore your actions will be influenced, compelled either by the outer or compelled by the inner. Fear is the instrument of compulsion, and compulsion exists only when there is no understanding, when intelligence is not functioning normally.

What are you trying to do with these values, through both the outer and inner compulsion? You want to reconcile the present moment with everything you know in and around you; you want to go along in the same old way, to have masters, teachers, gurus, your worship, your rites, your ceremonies, your customs, your traditions, your philosophies, your methods of thinking and feeling.

That is what you want, to keep the past in the present and you want to reconcile all that with the ever-changing new, with what is in the moment.

The psychological mind, which is the instrument and result of desire, fear, is repeatedly trying to make itself secure through beliefs, hopes, illusions, knowledge, ideals, patterns, which are for the most part attempts to hide your fears. Functionally, you are repeatedly trying to overcome fear through "emotion," that which you call love. You are trying to overcome fear through reason, analysis; and also you are trying to overcome fear by inhibiting or prohibiting it. Or you accept fear as a fundamental part of life, in order to enable you to put up with it. Often you sanction fear, and use it to control and to direct your actions.

Hence you use the cloaks of fear, such as ideals, beliefs, etc., and the instruments of fear, such as power, love, reason, to escape or get rid of fear. The past, the content of limited consciousness, is ever trying to overcome the future; habit proceeds to make the unknown into the known, the habitual, so that fear may cease. Thus the constant conflict of desire and fear is always present. The process is to absorb to be certain, to be satisfied, and when that is not possible the mind resorts to satisfying explanations, theories, beliefs. Thus death, the unknown, is made into the known; truth, the unconquerable, is made into the attainable; reason, which is unreliable, is held sacred; desire, which is destructive, is worshipped; and habit, which is deadening and limiting, becomes the normal way of life for all.

So this desire for security through keeping and reconciling the past in the present creates fear and habit. Fear is the root of this habit-forming mechanism. You must understand its process. To understand the mechanism of escape through habit, you must find concealed motive—the motive that drives you to a certain action, which brings in its wake what you call experience. In this process of experiencing, living, there is the gradual formation of the will. Now there is no divine will, but only the plain will of desire, the will to succeed, to be satisfied, to be. This will is a resistance. This will is the fruit of fear, which guides, chooses, justifies, disciplines. Through it you create one resistance after another, such as ideals, love, God, truth.

It is not possible to overcome fear either by desire or by what you call "emotion," which revolves around the "self," for emotion is really another form of desire.

Desire and vital emotion are two different and distinct processes. Desire is entirely of the mind and is always accompanied by fear. Vital emotion, the integral expression of one's whole being, is devoid of fear. Desire must always produce fear, and vital emotion has no fear in it at any time, for it contains the intensity of one's whole being. Vital emotion cannot conquer desire for vital emotion is a state of fearlessness, which can be experienced only when desire, with its fear and will of satisfaction, ceases. Vital emotion has no fear, for fear, as desire, is of the mind. Vital emotion is of a wholly different character, quality, dimension.

You cannot overcome fear by love. To overcome fear through

another force, which you call love, is not possible. For the desire to overcome fear is born of desire itself, of the mind itself, and what you call love is not love. Fear cannot be transmuted into love. It remains fear even though you try to reason it away, even though you may try to cover it up by calling it love.

Trying to inhibit, prohibit fear does not eradicate the cause of fear, but only produces further factors of disturbance and suffering. You will not discover the deep cause of fear by merely analyzing each fear. Thought cannot free itself from the root cause of fear by mere dissection of the various forms of fear. There is no remedy or substitution for fear, except the understanding of the cause of fear itself.

Psychological mind, which is desire, cannot destroy part of itself. This is what you are trying to do when you talk of "getting rid" of fear. When you ask, "How am I to get rid of fear? What am I to do about the various forms of fear?" you are wanting to know how to overcome one set of desires by another, which only perpetuates fear.

The psychological mind is a battlefield of its own desires, fears, values and so whatever effort it makes to destroy fear, that is to destroy itself, is utterly vain. The part that desires to get rid of fear, is ever seeking satisfaction; fear is trying to overcome that which has been the instrument of fear. Desire, creating fear in its search for security, tries to conquer that fear, but desire itself is the cause of fear. Desire cannot destroy itself, nor can fear overcome itself. All effort of the mind to rid itself of fear is born of desire. Thus the mind is caught in its own vicious circle of effort. Struggle exists so long as desire in any form continues.

As long as the mind desires security, there must be fear, and the attempt to escape from it only increases and strengthens the process. If the mind can free itself from the desire for security, then fear ceases. One can wholly eliminate fear, for it is not a fundamental part of life. This discriminative power of desire, choice, must cease and this can happen when one understands, inwardly feels, the blind effort of the psychological intellect. We must understand deeply the inward nature of the mind itself, the significance of the "I" process. Until one frees oneself from the mechanical—the will process—there cannot be the spontaneous, the real. When the mind neither accepts nor rejects fear, neither attempts to escape it, nor tries to transmute it, only then can there be the possibility of its cessation. When the mind is not caught in the conflict of opposites, then it is able to discern, without choice, the whole significance of the "I" process. No one is going to free you from fear, except yourself. No erection of churches, creation of gods, or images, no prayers, no worship, no ceremonies, no teachers, no gurus, no reasoning processes are going to give you that inward understanding and tranquility.

What we have to become are individuals who are certain of their salvation in themselves, who are strong, certain of their purpose and not looking for external comfort, external authority, external encouragement. To be so concentrated requires constant thoughtfulness.

If you really desire to discover the root of fear and so liberate yourself from it, you must become aware of the motive and purpose of your every action. Its cause must be self-discovered and so understood and dissolved through your own strenuous self-awareness. To trace fear through its many subtle ways, there must be the intense and burning desire to uncover fear, which means you must be willing to lose completely all self-interest. You must lose all sense of egotism.

As fear cannot allow you to be yourself, how then are you to overcome all fear? How are you to free yourself from all fear whether conscious or unconscious? If you are unconscious of fear, become conscious of it. Become aware of your thoughts and actions and soon you will be conscious of fear. You must be aware of the whole process of the will, of its struggles, its escapes, its miseries.

The motive power behind the will is fear. When you begin to realize this, the mechanism of habit intervenes, offering new escapes, new hopes, new gods. It is at this precise moment, when the mind begins to interfere with the realization of fear, that there must be great awareness not to be drawn off, not to be distracted by the offerings of the intellect, for the mind is subtle and cunning.

Until you free yourself from the mechanical, there cannot be the spontaneous, the real. What frees you from the mechanical is the deep observation of the process of the will, being one with it, without any desire to be free from it.

But your difficulty is to come to the point when you can look at the process of the will without fear. It can be done when there is no sense of "me" as being important. There is only one problem when you do not accept things as they are, and that is fear. Fear exists only in relationship to something—that something comes into being when you try to curb it—when you give it a name. When you name something that you want or do not want, or that you like or do not like, or some other inner state such as "I am wrong," "I am happy," "I want to keep my job," "I want to be liked," "I do not want to pay that bill," "I do not like Mr. Smith," you establish a relationship between yourself and the thing you label. You give it a neurological as well as a psychological significance and hence engender fear. You create the first psychological escape.

But if you do not name it, but simply regard it, look at it—then you will have a different relationship to it. Then it is not far away from you, it is you. If you do not give it a name—the observer is the observed. Then the sense of fear is absent. When you are no longer naming a thing of which you are afraid, then you are that thing. When you are that thing, there is no problem.

You can understand anything only when you look at it. You cannot look at it if you condemn it, or give it a name, or justify it, or identify yourself with it. You can understand it only when you are passively aware of what it is.

So if you are in psychological pain, look at it, live with it, and don't try to transform it into something else. Let it be exactly as it is. If you are in misery, physical or psychological, look at it as it is and try to understand it, by not wishing it to be different, but by being entirely with it, just as it is.

When there is deep thinking, passive awareness, vital emotion, you dissolve the projection of fear. Then you are face-to-face with fear. Then only can you resolve the cause of fear. When all avenues of escape have been thoroughly understood and thus destroyed, when every door of escape is closed, then you are face-to-face with the root of fear; only then can the mind liberate itself from the clutch of fear.

When you feel fear, face it. Then through tolerant observation of fear, through being aware of every facet of fear, fear is allowed to unfold itself, by following it through without identification, with kindly detachment. You must allow yourself to be silent, negative, without any exception. Then there comes creative understanding, which alone dissolves the cause of fear. When there is only fear, without any hope of escape, in its darkest moments, in the utter solitude of fear, there comes from within itself, as it were, the light that will dispel it.

Then you will find that the liberation from desire is the conquering of fear. And when you have no fear you really begin to live, neither hoping for salvation in the future, nor looking to the dead past for your strength—but because you have no fear you live in the moment, in the now.

There will always be fear as long as you do not realize that for every action, and the result of that action, for every desire, and the fulfillment of that desire, you are wholly responsible. If you come to this full realization, fear of every kind will disappear, because you, the individual, will be absolutely master of yourself.

CHAPTER 25

Limitations

*We cannot discover our limitations by analyzing the past.
To discover the false standards and barriers of the past you
must act with full awareness in the present. In that awareness
you discover your hindrances, your enclosures, authorities,
creeds, dogmas, ideals, beliefs, opinions, judgments. All these
are limitations. Experiment and you will see. Thought can free
itself from its own limitations by becoming intensely aware
of its own processes, possessive love, and its craving
for its own certainty.*

Look about you and you will see that man is imprisoned by innumerable walls, walls of religion, walls created by his own conclusion, opinions, concepts, by his ambitions, aspirations, fears, hopes, prejudices, hate, love, by his incessant search for security, through ideas, things and people. He is held within these barriers, limited by the colored maps of national boundaries, racial antagonisms, class struggles and cultural distinctions. You see man throughout the world imprisoned, enclosed by limitations, walls of his own creation. Through these enclosures he is trying to express what he feels and what he thinks. Within these he experiences joy and sorrow. Within these walls he is trying to function, sometimes successfully and sometimes with hideous struggle. The man who succeeds in making himself comfortable in the prison, we call a success, whereas the man who cannot succeed, we call a failure. Success and failure are both within the walls of the same prison.

You need to understand that what you call action is but movement within the limitation of environment; movement confined to a fixed idea, a fixed prejudice, a fixed belief, a fixed dogma, creed. It is a reaction in consciousness. So the more you act, the less intelligent and free you become because you have always this fixed point of safety, security, from which you act.

This prison, in which you mostly unconsciously live, is the result of your desires, cravings, which are expressed through your will—the will to gain satisfaction, the will to survive. The search for immortality has developed a consciousness, which maintains and demands individualized action. It keeps you constantly in conflict with your environment, society. Behind it all, there is the idea of gain. Each of us has many limitations, limitations of which we are unconscious. We cannot discover these limitations by analyzing the past. To discover the false standards and barriers of the past you must act with full awareness in the present. In that awareness you discover your hindrances, your enclosures, authorities, creeds, dogmas, ideals, beliefs, opinions, judgments. All these are limitations. Experiment and you will see. Thought can free itself from its own limitations by becoming intensely aware of its own processes, possessive love, and its craving for its own certainty.

We talk about brotherhood, and yet we are nationalists. Nationalism and brotherhood cannot exist together. We talk of brotherly love, yet send men off to wars; we talk of kindness toward our fellow men, yet exploit them every day; we talk of equality, yet have class differences. We talk about the unity of man and yet keep our particular religions, our particular prejudices, our class distinctions. Many seek distinctions, concessions, government honors. Those who turn to distinction in religious activity are also men of the world and their self-glorification is just the same, only more subtle. With their hierarchical distinctions, their exclusiveness, they also are trying to become noble, to attain honors and degrees, but in a religious environment. You are possessive yet talk about freedom from possessions. You talk of tolerance, and yet are becoming more and more exclusive. To all this you are insensitive, so your society is based on hypocrisy. Your life is filled with blindness. All your acts are quite the opposite to your words. Whether you do this consciously or unconsciously is of no importance. The fact is that you do it. If you do it consciously, with fully awakened interest, then at least you are doing it without hypocrisy. Then you know what you are doing. Then there is some hope that you will find out that this process leads nowhere.

We have built up through the centuries an environment of illusions, such as authority, imitativeness, beliefs, ideals, opinions, which give us many opportunities of subtle escapes and illusions. Illusion can never create human unity nor awaken that love, which alone can bring peace.

Through the centuries we have built up a system—the possessive system. This possessive system is based on security. Each one of us is responsible for this system of acquisition, gain, power, authority and imitation. We have made laws based on our selfishness, and we have become slaves to those laws. Our present laws and ethics are founded on the desire to hold and control. They are born of possessiveness, acquisitiveness and separateness; part of the present system of exploitation and self-protection. We have principles and rules to restrain, guide, control and direct our lives. Where we wish to dominate man, we have "principles" with which to suppress him, force him to comply with our wishes. We have reform measures ,which are compulsory, used to dominate, force, and compel man to conform to ideologies based on fear, insecurity, authority.

Real reform, real radical change of thought, does not lie in the patchwork of social reforms, religions, morals, but in seeing the absurdity of them.

When you become aware of yourself, you will find that you are in a state of contradiction, of wanting and not wanting, of loving and hating, and so on. Thoughts and actions born of these psychological contradictions are considered to be positive. But is it positive when thought contradicts itself? Because of your religious training you are certain that you must not kill but you find yourself supporting or finding reasons for killing when your government demands it. In a state of self-contradiction, thought ceases. You conform to outside influences. You do not think, you react. So let us discover if we think at all or exist merely in a state of contradiction. Can such a state be positive? Not knowing ourselves profoundly, how can there be agreement, assertion or denial? How can we, in this state, assume that we are right or wrong? We cannot assume anything, can we? Our morality, our positive action is based on this self-contradiction, and so we are incessantly active, longing for peace, and creating war. We desire happiness, yet cause sorrow; we long for love, yet we hate. If our thinking is self-contradictory, it is valueless and useless for adequate relationship, for adequate action.

CHAPTER 26

Desire

Desire is not an emotion; desire is the result of the mind that is ever seeking satisfaction. The motive behind all desire is to be satisfied at any cost. If it is thwarted in one direction, it seeks to achieve its purpose in another. Desire is the motive power behind all effort, by whatever name you may like to call it— success, wealth, righteousness, the good, godliness.

Few people are aware of the real cause of their suffering. They only desire to escape from that suffering. This is particularly evident in our moral and religious systems, which throughout the world are based on evasion, the searching for mediators and comforters. Because we are seeking escape from our suffering, we create systems and authorities, which will give us comfort and shelter. To avoid suffering, our sense of inadequacy and emptiness, we have created a complex of desires.

There is the desire to become, to succeed, to find truth, reality, God. There is the positive desire to be something, and the negative desire not to be something. Desire is always for something; it is dependent, and being dependent there is always uncertainty and this uncertainty breeds fear. If you are attached there is agony, suffering, and from that you learn that attachment gives pain. So you desire not to be attached, and cultivate the negative quality, detachment. Desire is always prompting you to be this or that.

Desire cannot exist by itself, it must be in relationship to something. You can observe this in your daily psychological reactions.

Desire creates and maintains the self, the me and mine. The self, the consciousness of me and mine is built up through desire. The self is a series of thought-feelings not only of the past, but of the influence of the past on the present.

Through the desire to be satisfied, the mind develops its own technique of resistance and nonresistance, which is the will. From desire springs reason, conclusion, action. The values and moralities resulting from desire are based on the will to survive, to be satisfied, to be free of suffering. Desire is not an emotion; desire is the result of the mind that is ever seeking satisfaction. The motive behind all desire is to be satisfied at any cost. If it is thwarted in one direction, it seeks to achieve its purpose in another. Desire is the motive power behind all effort, by whatever name you may like to call it—success, wealth, righteousness, the good, godliness. All effort, all the power of the mind is directed toward seeking its satisfaction. Thus, to find satisfaction becomes the mechanical habit of the mind.

Desire is the root of all selfishness and of all ignorance. It expresses itself through authority, mystery, miracle, pride of position, family, knowledge, talent, capacity, things. It is the cause of all frustration and hopelessness, of our misery, confusion, conflict, war. Desire makes life an ugly struggle, one of continual strife, no peace. Desire is the self-imposed limitation of man, it is the basic barrier to real living.

Conflict arises between the conditioning influences of desire and the swift, lively current of relationship. It is not, as most people think, relationship that is limiting. It is desire, conscious or unconscious, that is ever creating friction in relationship.

Greed, craving, is the demand for gratification. Greed breeds envy and hate. Imitation is the result of envy. Our social structure is based on envy and imitation. Greed, the demand for gratification in its many forms, pits man against man, bringing disunion and contention.

Only through understanding the process of craving, greed, by constant alertness, by becoming aware of it, is there the possibility of thought freeing itself from it. To be able to look newly on the problem of greed, we must be fully aware of the fallacy of mere social legislation against it. We must also be aware of the religious compensatory attitudes that we have developed. If you are no longer seeking religious compensation for unfulfilled greed, or if you are not caught up in the false hope of legislation against greed, then you will begin to understand a different process of dissolving greed. But this requires a strenuous earnestness without emotionalism, without the escapes of the cunning intellect.

We must understand the subtleties of greed. Merely adjusting ourselves to our environment to bring peace in our relationship with the family, friends, the world, will be in vain. In adjustment the self, the instrument of craving, is still the chief actor. Merely to suppress or deny the object of craving does not free thought from greed. Nor can you destroy greed through legislation—you may be able to destroy one form of greed through compulsion. But it will, inevitably, take another form, which will again create the same conflicts.

There are those who think greed or craving can be destroyed through intellectual or emotional ideals; through religious dogmas and creeds. This cannot be, for self-forgetfulness is not a lasting remedy for the conflict of greed. Religions have offered compensation for greed but compensation covers up the cause. The conflict and sorrow caused by greed are still there.

We see we are caught up in greed and also perceive, at least intellectually, the effect of greed. How then can thought free itself from its own self-created cravings? This is brought about through watching the actions of daily life. By becoming keenly aware of the process of craving, there comes into being a different type of understanding, which is not the product of the will to achieve, the will of craving and conflict. This understanding brings freedom from greed.

CHAPTER 27

Attachment

*You understand attachment only when the mind and heart
are not escaping through the idea of "detachment." This
understanding is not brought about through time, but only
through the realization that in attachment itself there is pain
as well as transient joy.*

The desire for security creates attachment. You get attached to those things, ideas and people, which you believe will give you this security. Experiencing self-satisfaction creates attachment. Experiencing pain, dissatisfaction, creates detachment. If you are attached and are satisfied with your state, you experience no disturbance. Only in times of pain and suffering do you want the opposite, which you think will give you relief. If you are attached to a person and there is peace and quiet, everything moves smoothly until something happens that gives you pain. Then you are in conflict. You want to be detached and at the same time you want to be attached. In this conflict, there is pain. Take for example a husband and wife; in their possessiveness, in their love, there is complete happiness. Life goes smoothly until something happens—he may leave her, or she may fall in love with another. Then there is pain. Then you say, "Let me be detached." Or there may be intense conflict over some issue, behavior or problem, which creates great pain. In this pain you want to be free of the person who gives you pain, while at the same time you want to keep and possess him or her. Possession creates jealousy, continual watchfulness, a never-ending strife and struggle. Your attachment brings strife in relationship. You say, "Let me find a way, a means, by which I shall not suffer." So your detachment is merely a running away from pain. In attachment there is conflict that awakens you, stirs you, and in order not to be awakened you long for detachment. You go through life wanting the exact opposite of that which gives you pain, and that wanting is but an escape from the thing in which you are caught. But if you should love again, you repeat the same thing. Again, when you experience pain in attachment you desire the opposite. That is what every human being experiences.

You seek detachment from suffering rather than the understanding of the cause of suffering. When you suffer through possessiveness, you try to develop the opposite. You become "detached" in order not to be hurt, and this opposite you call virtue. If you really discover the cause of suffering, if you understand it deeply, with your whole being, the mind will be free to love fully and completely and not fall into the prison of the opposites. If you perceive with your entire being the whole significance of attachment, then you do not get involved in attachment or detachment. The mere pursuit of detachment does not reveal the shallowness of attachment. You understand attachment only when the mind and heart are not escaping through the idea of "detachment." This understanding is not brought about through time, but only through the realization that in attachment itself there is pain as well as transient joy. So it is not a matter of acquiring detachment. It is a matter of seeing the futility of attachment when you suffer in attachment. In pain itself you realize the ending of pain. If you do not try to escape to the opposite, then that very pain will free you from both attachment and detachment.

You think you grow from attachment to detachment, renunciation, through the constant shock of experience. This you call progress, development of character. This is not progress. Where there is attachment, there is fear, but the freedom from fear is not the reward of nonattachment. Suffering makes one decide to be utterly detached, but this detachment is really a form of protection against suffering.

Become aware of your attachments. The majority of you have something, love, possessions, ideals, beliefs, to which you are attached and want to protect. Any one of these go to make up that resistance, the "I," the "me." It is futile to ask how to get rid of the "I," the "me," with its many layers of wants, fears, without fully comprehending the process of resistance, of self-protection. The very desire to free oneself from the "I" is but another and safer form of self-protection.

CHAPTER 28

Choice

*A wholly different approach is necessary to comprehend
the individuality of man. This approach lies through direct
discernment, through action not based on choice*

Choice is psychological selection by the intellect.

Choice exists where there is a duality. Choice is born of resistance. Choice is concerned with the opposites, a discrimination between what we consider the essential and the unessential, between right and wrong. It is based on like and dislike, on craving and ignorance, memory, self-protective promptings, tendencies, calculations, prejudice and continuous sensation. Choice loses all validity and prevents discernment. Choice creates conflict.

The conflict of choice arises when the intellect, with its fears and limitations of mine and another's, of merit and demerit, of failure and success, begins to project itself into the attempted solution of our human problems. If your action requires a choice, by being conditioned by the past, by fear or by environment, your action is incomplete.

It is prejudice that creates choice. Prejudice is a form of resistance. Prejudice is very deep-rooted—the prejudice of class, nationality, color, creed, religion, etc. These prejudices, which form the "I" process, will determine choice. We have many prejudices, subtle and gross. Each individual, being unique, sustains his own ignorance through his own desire, effort and choice. You must comprehend this self-active ignorance fully, in its entirety.

Our process of choice manifests as substitution, imitation, conformity and adjustment. You talk of searching for truth, but your search is really for substitutes, the desire for greater security and greater certainty. One doesn't search for truth, one lives it. When man searches for truth, there is fear and therefore increased conflict. When you are afraid you seek the opposite of fear, you choose a substitute which you call "courage." You are caught in the choice of opposites.

Our entire lives are a process of imitation and conformity. Our thought is the result of the past. Our being is founded on the past. Organically and in thought we are copies. Our environment political, social, religious positions are all copies. A copy, a thing put together, the self, can never understand that which is not made up. Public opinion, your family, friends, the doctor, the preacher, priest, the teacher, the politician, etc., say so and so, so you do it. You conform, you imitate. This does not mean that you must go against all convention; that you must impetuously do "whatever you like." Free yourselves from all imitation; question all values. It is only when the copy, the self, the "me" and "mine" ceases that you become really yourself.

A wholly different approach is necessary to comprehend the individuality of man. This approach lies through direct discernment, through action not based on choice. The dawning of turn does not lie in the choice of the essential as against the unessential. When you perceive the illusion of choice itself, that revelation is liberating, spontaneously destroying the illusion upon which the mind now nourishes itself. Being aware of this process of choice, of conflict between the opposites, there is a change of will, and this will is the result of choicelessness. So you must become aware of this process, and with that discernment there comes, not the development of an opposite, but the comprehension of reality.

CHAPTER 29

Beliefs

*When you say, "I believe," you limit thought, and turn belief
into a pattern, which guides and conducts your life, thus
allowing the mind–heart to become narrow, crystallized, and
incapable of adjustment to life and reality.*

Belief is part of ignorance. Whatever action springs from belief only further strengthens ignorance. Belief is an artificial thing. It is false. Belief is a hindrance. Mind cannot think completely, fully, if it is tethered to a belief. It can only think within the limited circle of that belief. Belief separates people. Belief indicates the incapacity to understand the present.

On what is belief based? On what are most ideals founded? If you consider, you will find that belief has for it motive either the idea of gain, reward, or it serves as a guide, a pattern. Either you have external ideals or principles or you have developed inner ideals and principles by which you are living. External principles are imposed by society, by tradition, by authority. They are based on fear. These are the principles that you are constantly using as your standard. "What will my neighbors think?" "What does public opinion maintain?" "What do the sacred books or teachers say?" Or you develop an inner belief, an inner law, which is nothing more than a reaction to the outer; you develop an inner belief to guide you, an inner principle, based on the memory of experience, on reaction.

Religion, with its beliefs, its disciplines, its enticements, its hopes, its punishments, forces you toward "righteous" behavior, toward "brotherliness," toward "love." And since you are compelled, you obey the external authority. Or you react against the outer and begin to develop your own inner authority and follow that. Where there is a following of any authority, any ideal, inner or outer, there cannot be complete living.

A man whose thought-emotion is based on faith, and so on belief, must necessarily be unbalanced, for his belief is merely wish-fulfillment. When people say that they believe in reincarnation, in immortality, in God, they are but having emotional cravings, which to them become objectified concepts and "facts."

When you say, "I believe," you limit thought, and turn belief into a pattern, which guides and conducts your life, thus allowing the mind-heart to become narrow, crystallized, and incapable of adjustment to life and reality. With most people, belief becomes an escape from the conflict and confusion of life. Belief is based on escape, on frustration, on limitation. Belief prevents the mind-heart from dissolving its self-created ignorance.

When you bind life to beliefs and tradition, to codes of morality, you kill life. No belief is ever a living reality. The man who is truly living needs no beliefs.

CHAPTER 30

Morality

One of the most illusory phases of our psychological self-protective way of life, the old, that which we are, is man's formulated and acquired morality. This moral process is the measure with which we give value to, qualify, and pass judgment upon man and everything in life. All things, animate or inanimate, all ideas, all feelings, all people, all behavior manifestations, all relationships, cosmic or mundane, are interpreted, evaluated, judged, termed and standardized through man's intellectually formulated moralistic methods and concepts. Man moralizes the factual as well as the psychological. Everything is tainted with psychological moralization. In so doing, he has formulated and developed the dual process of moral comparative thought. He has falsely given double value and qualities to everything, himself included, and he is caught in and between their artificial values and qualities. He has constructed a psychological tightrope along which no one does or can walk, a psychological trap for his own undoing. He has designated imaginary moral values and qualities to exist in himself and all other things and he considers them to be finalities, conditioning all people to accept and believe in them as realities. For example, man has conceived dualistic moral values of good and bad, right and wrong, superior and inferior. These are ill-conceived and transitory. He has committed himself to moral reactions of should and should not, be and not be, do and not do, give and take, and so on, whose ever-changing content keeps him in constant turmoil. He has assigned to himself dualistic moral qualities, such as sincerity and insincerity, loyalty and disloyalty, honesty and dishonesty, righteous and unrighteous, religious and irreligious, courageous and cowardly, respectful and disrespectful, patriotic and unpatriotic, and innumerable other dualistic moral qualities. All of these are formulated for his individual and collective security.

Actually, these opposites do not exist in man as such, for they are psychological instruments for the purpose of self-protection. These moral assignments and their pervasive influence have been man's undoing. He lives in constant contradiction, floundering back and forth trying to fulfill them. From ancient times these moralized procedures have been formulated by all races of men and in all parts of the world. Each of these races has had, and the present races do now have, their own special moral interpretations and procedures, which in great measure vary and contradict each other. Moral standards in one country often contradict the moral standards in another country. Actually there is no single moral standard for man existing on earth. Ideals, virtues, morality are not means to an end. No method, no discipline can bring about virtue. Virtue is a result of right action.

All men have been conditioned in some form of moral thought, in some form of ideals and moral behavior. This has been done to guide and control man's behavior in his relationship with others, and to protect him from himself and from others. But these psychological ideals and moral disciplines have, at best, been only temporary and partial restraints to man's behavior. They confirm the fact that man is truly his greatest tribulation. Nevertheless, all men have been told that when these manmade moral edicts have been fulfilled, some form of reward or happiness will be theirs, and when they fail in these commitments, they are unworthy and damned. Through fear, man has designated how both God and man should act. This artificial dualistic moral process has created in man a form of consciousness consisting of false thoughts and feelings of self-achievement; it has created self-importance and self-approbation when he has complied with these moral mandates, and a sense of failure and guilt when he has not complied.

Man moves back and forth between these two forms of negative thinking and feeling. No matter what he does, he is caught in it. He is never free of the sense of either doing right, psychological self-achievement, or of doing wrong, psychological failure. Every thought, every feeling in reaction is qualified in either one or the other of these two forms of response. Man is in a constant state of critical judgment of himself or others.

As everyone is conditioned in these concepts of reward for fulfillment and punishment for failure, they form the guiding part of our psychological consciousness. As such, we are these concepts and through them we live and have our being. All that we do, all that we can do, and all that we expect to do, will produce within us reactions of either one phase or the other of self-glory or blight, exaltation or stigma. When we think we have fulfilled the manmade moral code, it will produce artificial subjective self-importance, artificial self-consciousness. When we have violated the manmade moral code, it will produce artificial, derogatory subjective self-consciousness. No matter what we do, we are this illusory moral consciousness, and it is this we use in our search for self-knowledge. In so doing we destroy the real, the new, qualifying everything with illusory moral concepts, thereby creating self-deception and self-made subjective self-consciousness.

How has our present moral process failed us in our search for self-knowledge? The moral process promises you a reward for your efforts, hence it has created an attitude of mind of expectant reward or gain. Being this formulated type of consciousness, you have approached the search for self-knowledge with an attitude of expectant achievement. You have come to it with an attitude of acceptance or rejection in keeping with the objective of gain. You expect to obtain fulfillment and security. This protective expectant attitude of mind is the product of the moral means in which you have been conditioned to meet all experiences in life. So the state of your consciousness is one of conditioned expectancy. As you meet all experiences with guarded and expectant achievement, in your search for self-knowledge you have used this expectant attitude of mind in exactly the same way as you do in your approach to other knowledge. This psychological moral process is entirely false, and it defeats its own purpose.

You have not given much consideration to the fact that very few of your thoughts, or the thinking-feeling processes through which you live and have your being, really belong to you, though you call them your own. For the most part, you are but a mirror reflecting the ideas of others. You have very little of your own with which to meet life, and that with which you do meet it has been obtained in the course of your conditioning and self-reconditioning and belongs almost in its entirety to those who have gone before. You are an imitator, an intellectual parrot, a tape recorder, who lives through a conditionally acquired consciousness, the substance of which is not your own. You are an automaton, a mechanism of psycho-emotional reaction only, whose reactions stem from manmade customs, standards, knowledge, information, methods, ideas, conclusions, opinions, religions, theories, and so on.

Obviously, we do not have issue with the actual facts of life established by man. We are concerned with the fictitious formulas through the imaginative process of psychological duality, which keeps man in a constant state of contradiction.

The present-day morality, the discipline that you now practice, is based on the search and protection for your own safety and security. It is a closed system, which acts as a covering to hold the individual within the group. The individual is treated as if he must be kept in a cage of morality. We have become slaves to individual and group morality. Each one of us has contributed to this system. We have created static religions with their static gods, dead images, petrified thoughts. This morality has become so powerful, so compulsive, that most individuals unconsciously live in fear of breaking away from it, and imitate the prevailing rules and conduct.

The everyday morality is really immorality, and the world is caught in this immorality. Various forms of acquisitiveness, exploitation and killing are honored by governments and by religious organizations and are the basis of accepted morality. In all this there is no love but only fear, which is covered over by constant repetition of idealistic words, which prevent us from seeing our fear.

You may talk about love and brotherhood on Sundays, but on Mondays you exploit others. Religion, morality, discipline, merely act as a cover for hypocrisy. Such a morality is immoral. You ruthlessly seek economic security, out of which is born a morality suited for that purpose.

So let us look at this structure of morality and discipline that we have built up and which is exploiting us, which is destroying human intelligence. Are there not wars, ruthless exploitation, rivalry, utter chaos in the world? If you examine this structure of morality and discipline, with great care and without prejudice, you will begin to understand and develop that true morality, which cannot be systematized.

There is the morality of the ideal. The ideal is to love one another, not to kill, not to exploit, and so on. But our actions, our conduct is not based on this idea. The ethic of our everyday existence, the morality of our social relationships is based fundamentally on acquisitiveness, on fear, on self-protectiveness. As long as these exist, how can there be true morality, true relationship of the individual with people, his government, with society? As long as each one is isolating himself through fear, acquisitiveness, egotistic cravings, beliefs, ideals, how can there be true relationship with another?

For you to be truly moral, that is, for you to have relationship with another, with society, your immorality must cease. You must be free of the present immorality. You have to become intensely aware of this prison, of this continual building up of securities, comforts and escapes, in which the mind is engaged. When you are fully aware of the cause of this, then the mind itself begins to discern the true manner of acting in the very moment of experience. Then morality becomes purely individual. It cannot be made a means of exploitation. Knowing the cause and being continually aware of it, the mind itself begins to break through the covering of self-protective morality, which has been so crushing, so destructive of intelligence. When the mind frees itself from this center of limited consciousness, then there comes the exquisite and delicate adjustment of life, which does not demand rules and regulations, but which is consummately intelligent, expressing itself in the integrated action of true discernment. In that awareness, which is the awakening of intelligence, the mind breaks through to the flow of reality. This cannot become a static religion, a means of exploitation, nor can it be petrified in the prayer books of priests.

Many people want to know what God is, what truth is, what eternal life is. God, truth, or whatever you choose to call reality, cannot be described. The man who describes what truth or God is does not know truth. When truth is put in the cage of words, then truth is no longer a living reality. It is vain to inquire whether there is a God. Both belief and nonbelief in God prevent understanding.

CHAPTER 31

God

If you understand life, if you grasp the deep significance of living, then life itself is God, not some superintelligence apart from you. But this demands great penetration of thought, not the seeking of satisfaction or explanation.

Why do we want to believe in God? What is belief? You do not believe in something obvious, like sunshine, like the person sitting next to you; you do not have to believe. Your belief in God is a hope, an idea, a preconceived longing, which may not have anything to do with reality.

The belief that there is a divinity that can help man is one of man's greatest hindrances. The idea that some miracle will change us; that some divine or external influence will bring about changes in ourselves and in the world is an illusion. Thinking that a divine power is going to do everything for us leads to irresponsibility in action.

We have believed in God for centuries and centuries, yet we have created a terrible world. The savage and the highly civilized priest both believe in God. The primitive kills with bows and arrows; the civilized priest blesses warships, bombers, soldiers and prays for success in battle. Both of them "believe." Then there are the nonbelievers who resort to liquidating those who stand in their way. Clinging to belief or to an ideology does not do away with killing, with oppression and exploitation. On the contrary, there have been and continue to be terrible, ruthless wars, destruction and persecution in the name of peace, in the name of God.

Religion, God and immortality are means of escape. Religion has helped man to escape from conflict, the suffering of life, and therefore from understanding it. When you are in conflict with life, exploitation, jealousy, cruelty and so on, you unconsciously try to escape. You do not fundamentally desire to understand—for to understand demands intelligent action. As you are unwilling to make the effort, you escape to ideals, values, beliefs. So immortality, God and religion have merely become illusory shelters.

If you deeply think over this whole idea of seeking God you will see that in trying to seek God you are subtly, cunningly escaping from the conflict of life. If you understand life, if you grasp the deep significance of living, then life itself is God, not some superintelligence apart from you. But this demands great penetration of thought, not the seeking of satisfaction or explanation.

If you were really aware of truth as you are conscious of flowers, fresh air, clouds and sunlight, then your whole life, your whole conduct, your whole behavior would be different. At present, your belief has nothing to do with your daily life; so whether you believe in God or not is immaterial. They are both the same. The discovery of truth, God, demands great awareness. What is important is not the assertion of belief or disbelief but the recognition of the hindrances created by the lack of intelligence. So, to discover truth, God, the mind must be free from all the hindrances, which have been created throughout the ages based on self-protection and security.

You cannot approach this problem, whether there is a God or not with any particular prejudice, for or against. What you can do is let the mind free itself from all illusions, from all fears, prejudices and longings.

You can discover whether there is truth, God, immortality, only in the completeness of action itself, not through any belief whatsoever, not through any external authority. Only in action is reality revealed, only in the fullness of self-awareness without identification.

When there is that sense of God, truth, you do not belong to any religion, to any group of people, to any family. It is only when you cling to the belief in God that you become "religious" and submit yourself to all the absurdities and cruelties, to exploitation and suffering. As long as the mind is not vulnerable to the movement of life, to the swift lively current of life, there cannot be reality. Mind must be utterly naked, vulnerable, unprotected, to follow the wandering of truth.

If a man is truly desirous to free himself, let him understand the cause of sorrow and conflict. In the very understanding of conflict and suffering, when all securities and supports have become useless, when you are face-to-face with life, there is God.

CHAPTER 32

Organized Religion

*The function of real religion is to uphold what is true.
Organized religion, to exist at all, must and does become
an adjunct of the state and of the status quo and thereby loses its
true function. It becomes another means of oppression
and division.*

Religion as an organized system of belief, creed, dogma, authority, is based on fear and on the desire for security. This form of religion forces the individual to conform to a certain pattern, which he is made to believe is for his own good. This is done through fear, faith, dogma, creed, ceremonies and pageantry. The escape of the individual through illusions gives immense satisfactions, encouragement and happiness. This sensation and thrill we generally call religious experience. If you examine closely you will see that these experiences are self-evolved compensations for suffering.

Your lives are weighed down by routine, regimentation, drudgery, long and exhausting hours of work, difficult economic and social problems. You try to find justification and compensation by joining organized religions, spiritual groups and through metaphysical teachings. In your search for God, you seek masters, teachers, you participate in ceremonies, rituals, creeds and dogmas. These are not religious activities. They are for the most part, the pursuit of sensation, pleasure. No true spirituality can be born of imitation. Virtue is not born of disciplines, and false worship. It exists when there is self-knowledge, which releases creative action.

Through religion many seek what is called immortality, a security in the hereafter. Those who promise immortality become their guides, their teachers and authorities. Out of their own desire for egotistic continuance, they create their own exploiters.

Organized religion is a system of thought that holds the individual in the groove of a particular pattern. This inner system is both cruel and exploitative. It contains beliefs, ideas, percepts, long-established by tradition. Religion forces the individual through faith and illusory hope to think and act along one particular line, blindly and unintelligently, with the help of the exploiting priests, preachers, and functionary members of organizations.

Many think that their own specialized religion conquering all others will bring happiness to man. There are hundreds of religious sects, each competing, proselytizing. Do you think any specialized religion, whether it be Hinduism, Buddhism or Christianity, will bring peace? You must set aside all organized religions and discover reality for yourself.

The function of real religion is to uphold what is true. Organized religion, to exist at all, must and does become an adjunct of the state and of the status quo and thereby loses its true function. It becomes another means of oppression and division.

Unless you become religious in the true sense of the word, you will be irreligious, and therefore responsible for wars and economic disaster, oppression, killing and misery. We are using the words "real religion" not in any particular sense. Religion stands above all names and labels.

CHAPTER 33

Discipline

*Is it possible to discipline yourself in order to become
spontaneous? No. Discipline implies a pattern, a mold.
All of man's self-imposed limitations, his disciplines, or
self-made resistances act as enormous hindrances to his
understanding of life.*

Discipline as we know it today is based on the individual's search and protection for his own safety, security, through religion, morality and economic exploitation of others.

Discipline imposed from without by society, by leaders, and discipline imposed by personal desire, must inevitably destroy individual fulfillment. Such discipline, compulsion, conformity, postpones the inevitable problem of individual fear with its many illusions.

You give many reasons for disciplining yourself. There is the desire to protect yourself by achievement, by trying to become wiser, nobler, by finding a master, by becoming virtuous, by following principles, ideals, by wanting and craving for truth, for love and so on. All these indicate the presence of fear. The noble reason is but the coverup of this innate fear.

Most of us are caught up in the process of trying to overcome, to run away from circumstances, environment. We do not try to find out what environment means, what its cause is, its significance, its value. Suppression is the gross form of the subtler self-discipline, which is repression. Both suppression as well as self-discipline are adjustments to environment. Both are based on fear. Suppression and self-discipline are psychological instruments of resistance, substitutes for understanding. All overcoming is but substitution. We must realize that in substitution there is no understanding and therefore there can only be further sorrow.

Momentarily we may find a way that will put the mind to sleep. You say to yourself, "I must begin to discipline myself. I must learn to be more concentrated. I must practice awareness, develop certain virtues, act in a certain manner. I must become a better person." You conceive a pattern of what is good, or it has been imposed on you by tradition and education. If this is the ideal, the pattern for life's conduct that you pursue, through self-imposed discipline, then what is happening to your thoughts and emotions? You are forcing them, violently or lovingly, to conform, and thereby are merely establishing a new habit in place of the old. Habit is of the mind, of the will. It conceals fear without doing away with it. Thus intellect, the will, is controlling and shaping morality; it is will, based on the desire to protect yourself. It is born of fear.

Is it possible to discipline yourself in order to become spontaneous? No. Discipline implies a pattern, a mold. All of man's self-imposed limitations, his disciplines, or self-made resistances act as enormous hindrances to his understanding of life. Authority, which implies shaping, disciplining and imitation, a control, a conditioning, is a hindrance whether imposed externally or by inward effort and exertion. We must understand the whole process of the habit-forming mechanism, and not ask which discipline, which pattern or ideal is best. When the mind frees itself from this center of limited consciousness, which is based on self-aggrandizement, then there comes the exquisite and delicate adjustment to life, which does not demand rules, regulation, ideals or disciplines.

CHAPTER 34

Dependence

Dependence is the basis of most of our relationships.

Psychological dependence results in social misery and conflict. When you are poor inwardly, psychologically, spiritually, you think of enriching yourself through possessions. Every human being in the world needs food, clothes and shelter, but why is it that need has become such a complex, painful problem? It is because you use things for psychological purposes rather than for needs. You use things as a means for gratification and thereby give them far greater importance and worth than they have. When you use things because you need them, without being psychologically involved in them, there is an intelligent meeting of your needs, which is not based on gratification.

Psychological dependence upon ideas creates beliefs, ideals, dogmas, creeds, opinions and cults, which divide man against man. Dependence upon ideas creates authorities. Dependence upon an authority destroys understanding and further conditions the mind. Why do you depend upon a mediator to learn how not to be greedy, to have no ill will, to be compassionate? Why do you look at a distant ideal when understanding and love can be awakened only through human relationship? You love masters, gurus, gods, saviors, deified personalities, ceremonies, priests, authorities, because you do not know how to love human beings. Why is it that you depend so greatly on things or ideas with which to satisfy yourself? Is it not because relationship with others is so empty, devoid of real relationship?

Psychological dependence on individuals creates possessive love. Relationship is now based on dependence. We depend on another for economic and psychological satisfaction, happiness, and well-being. All psychological dependence creates fear. This fear breeds a new possessiveness, which in turn results in friction, suspicion, frustration. Economic dependence on another can perhaps be eliminated through legislation and proper organization, but we are referring especially to that psychological dependence on another, which is the outcome of craving for personal satisfaction and happiness. You feel in this possessive relationship, enriched, creative and active. You feel your own little flame of being increased by another and so in order not to lose this source of completeness, possessive fears come into being with all their resulting problems. When you love another possessively, your passion and jealousies are aroused. You find sorrow and conflict in this relationship, and because you cannot resolve this ache you try to run away from it. You then seek detachment from the pain of attachment.

The complex problem in relationship is how to love without dependence, without friction and conflict; how to conquer the desire to isolate yourself, to withdraw from the cause of conflict. If you depend for your happiness on another, on society, or on environment, they become essential to you, so you cling to them. You violently oppose any alteration of these because you depend upon them for your psychological security and comfort.

Though intellectually you may see that life is a continual process of flux, of mutation, necessitating a constant change, yet emotionally or sentimentally you cling to the established and comforting values; hence there is a constant battle between change and the desire for permanency.

All dependence reveals a lack of intelligence and creates suffering. When you rely psychologically on another, on a group, on a leader for your understanding, fear is created and a vicious cycle is started. Being fearful you depend on another, and depending on another you feel fearful.

Dependence, through fear, creates illusion and sorrow and prevents the understanding of the real. Thought dependent upon various beliefs and ideals prevents the understanding of human relationship, the unity of man.

When there is dependence there is emptiness, shallowness, insufficiency, and therefore sorrow and pain. The mind, which is intelligent, seeks no dependence, no security.

Since your relationship is based on possessive love you have to become aware in yourselves; its birth, its causes, its action. In becoming deeply aware of the process of possessiveness with its violence, fears, its reactions, there comes an understanding that is whole, complete. This understanding alone frees thought from dependence and possessiveness. It is within oneself that harmony in relationship can be found, not in another, not in environment. You must understand deeply that all psychological dependence, whether on things, on people or on ideas creates not only social but also personal conflict and sorrow. You must understand the complex causes of conflict and the desire to be free of them. This requires not the mere will to be free, but constant awareness in your daily life. But if that awareness is the outcome of a desire to achieve a certain result, the effort to be aware only produces further resistance and conflict.

CHAPTER 35

Fact

It is necessary to differentiate between the commonly accepted use of the word fact and the significance given to it in the "subject." The word fact, in its customary usage, is a word used to denote anything done. An act, a deed, is a fact. And also, anything declared to have happened, to have existed, or the asserting of something existing or done is considered to be a fact. Man considers these forms of fact to be reality, the actual. This is the generally accepted use of the word fact. Anything that does have or has had physical presence, form or action or that man psychologically designates and accepts to exist or have existed, whether verifiable or not, to him this is fact, truth. His physical fact is used to denote time, place, object, activity, etc., on the physical level and is simply objectively conceived, extrinsic fact. His psychological fact is used to denote mental, emotional and inner physical activities on the manmade psychological, intellectual level and is manmade subjectively conceived, extrinsic fact. As these facts are established through the registration of sensation, of which the psychic sensory thought is the criterion of their reality, their form of significance and acceptance as fact are only manmade psychological interpretations of his impressions of his inner and outer environment, or of that which he considers to have taken place in both the past and the present.

The word fact as used in the "subject" is of a more comprehensive, wider and vital nature. It is used to denote the existence of non-manmade, preestablished, unchangeable, designations, which are correlated to every expression of life and which will signify their true function and meaning. Our innate purpose is to be a channel through which these designations, intrinsic facts, creative manifestations, may find expression. And also it is essential to know that not we, but something not of us, can function through us, if given the opportunity, that will determine what is real, actual, and what should be done about it, what action to take.

Intrinsic fact reveals the true nature of physical facts, reveals the true nature of all manmade psychological facts. It reveals all psychological thoughts, and psycho-emotional feeling reactions. It reveals the true nature of relationship, unity, peace, happiness, illumination, understanding, intelligence, love.

We are not concerned with intrinsic fact for the purpose of gaining knowledge, or for the purpose of possession and use on our behalf. On the physical level our concern is to function in keeping with physical facts, to fulfill needs only, and not psychological wants. On the physiological level, to function in keeping with physiological facts, to fulfill the needs indicated, and to use the senses for what they were intended and not for psychological wants. On the psychological level, to face the falsity of psychological facts and be free of them. And on the intrinsic level to be the channel through which these facts may fulfill creative action. Fact is need, the essential in the now, no matter the level or the relationship or the factors involved in it or what it may bring. For intrinsic fact is its own designation and fulfillment. It is intrinsic cause, the means and end. It is action in the now. It has always existed, exists in the present, and will continue to exist. It is without beginning and end. It is incontrovertible, unchangeable, and stands alone, sufficient unto itself. It is devoid of fear, desire, and is without qualities. It reveals all falsities and indicates that which should be. It can be experienced on all levels, but the experience cannot be translated or given to another. At best, all translations will only be information about something. Fact does not demand a thought process. It is beyond the thought process and can be contacted only when the thought process ceases. Fact is of another dimension from thought, and it needs no confirmation, or defense, and it cannot be compared to anything. It is devoid of psychological sensation and interpretation. It needs no interpretation, for it signifies its meaning with clarity and without fail. It is directness, action, understanding. It is the whole. Intrinsic fact is the media through which man can adequately fulfill the purpose of his being, the release of creative action. This is his highest responsibility.

We must face the fact that we cannot continue to live as, and through, psychological desire, but must free ourselves from it, and live through fact and fact alone, need and need alone, that in consciousness we must become fact, its designations and actions.

Your initial and primary problem concerns psychological fact—what you are, what is, the content of the psychologically conditioned consciousness. Whenever you are confronted with a psychological fact your tendency is to protect yourself against it. Your first reaction is to accept it or reject it on the basis of whether you like it or dislike it. If you dislike it, you immediately alter or modify or change it in order to escape or avoid it. You are not concerned with the actual significance of the fact, only your psychological interpretation of it. By so doing you entirely miss the real knowledge contained in it and defeat the possibility of understanding yourself. Now there is nothing you should do about a fact, except face it, accept it and be it, then you are face-to-face with it. By so doing you can understand yourself for what you are and be free of that part of you and the problem. For to acknowledge, accept and be that which has been portrayed, then there is no longer a problem. When you are the fact, the problem no longer exists. To understand "what is" is to know the cause, hence be freed from it.

Your trouble is that you immediately start thinking about it, qualifying it, giving it a name, calling it fear, greed, vanity, cruelty, respectful, helpful and so on, and then you have to act on that, which takes you away from the real problem. You don't just sit with that which is going on inside your consciousness and understand it for what it is. Whenever you want to avoid fact, the thought process begins. But if you accept "what is," then the thought process is absent, and something else takes place. Quite a different process comes into being when you are not trying to find an answer, when you let go. Then there is a response, there is an intimation, because you are no longer obstructing fact by trying to find an answer. Then fact is present, then there is intelligence and understanding.

If through fact you can understand each thought, each feeling, and not resist it, not push it away, alter it, avoid it; if you can look at each thought from the outside or inside, as it arises, and uncover its meaning, then you will understand and act in accordance with fact. If you totally become the fact in thought and feeling, the fact will be resolved. Only facts not understood come back. Those which do not come back have been resolved through transcending the cause. If you do this, you will be aware of your falsities through fact and be free of them by being factual consciousness, its designation and action.

When experiencing through factual consciousness there is only a state of experiencing and not the experiencer apart from the experienced. There is only a constant state of experiencing—not the center, the "I," the "me," the memory, the intellect, experiencing, but only a state of experiencing. If there is not the entity that manifests through one quality or another such as envy, hatred, service, duty, suspicion, etc., but only the state of experiencing, then there is complete transformation.

So when there is experiencing of that which is vital, which is essential, which is real, which is the beginning of transformation, then the mind is quiet, without compulsion. And when the mind is quiet, it is capable of receiving. Then fact can be present. Creativeness can take place only when the psychological mind has come to that state when it is utterly still.

Through the awareness of the false elements of the duality process in yourself, the "what is" of your daily living, right relationship comes into being, bringing new responsibility. Out of this new responsibility comes new motivation, response and direction in living. An entirely new intent and aim are born, a vital need to know and be "what is"—clarity of endeavor becomes the need, to be constantly alert and factually responsive. Vital interest and enthusiasm are the earnest needs, to give yourself totally to understanding "what is." Vital interest and enthusiasm are born of need, fact.

CHAPTER 36

Responsibility

*So, through the awakening to and the understanding of
the false elements of the duality process in ourselves, a new
responsibility comes into being. With the significance of new
responsibility, the need for right relationship is born.*

When you come to the search for self-knowledge, you did not know the real significance of responsibility, what it is concerned with or in what manner it is fulfilled. Even now, though you are working on the subject, it is possibly more vague than real. Your present understanding of responsibility is formed of self-protective ideas and conclusions, upon psychological thought. It is with these concepts that you have applied yourself. Your concept of responsibility is no different than any other psychological process. The only difference are the ideas you use. In your present application of knowledge you are not different from the pacifist who adheres to the tenets of pacifism, upholding and advocating them as his responsibility. Nor are you any different from the nationalist who adheres to the policies of patriotism and organized killing, extolling, upholding and advocating them as his responsibility. We are all moving from the same basis with the self and its self-fulfillment as the motive. In this we are all alike, irresponsible and destructive.

Responsibility is concerned first with that to which one is responsible and, second, the fulfillment of action in keeping with that responsibility. "That to which one is responsible" is of primary significance for no matter what it may be, whether organized religion, military activity, business activity, marriage relationship, knowledge of the self, your behavior, if you accept the obligation it will be in keeping with the type of activity you have selected and you will carry out its demands. If it is military activity and patriotism, you will destroy and kill; if it is organized religion, you will sacrifice yourself and others for the "church," for the organization; if it is business, you will have to compete with all others in business and use whatever means possible to make a success of it, no matter whether you hurt to destroy others doing so. As long as you are purposely trying to protect yourself, your responsibility will be as variable as your endeavor. There is no common responsibility for all men in the psychological process. It is individual and therefore disruptive. In this process there is no true responsibility among men, there is only, underlying all his supposedly responsible behavior, the protection and achievement of the self. What he calls his "responsibilities" are but ideas for his own individual and collective security.

There is, however, a responsibility common to all men, a way of life in which, when fulfilled, will be responsible on all levels and to all things. But, before such responsibility can exist, it will first be necessary to know what that responsibility consists of and to what we are responsible.

Man through purposeful psychological endeavor cannot create a new and different means with which to understand and fulfill life. A new and different means can come about only through understanding the falsities that he now creates, uses, and through which he lives. Until this is done, that which is essential, creative, that which is need, fact, cannot be known. Creative fact exists, and we have to wake up to it. And for this to be, that which obstructs its manifestation, man's illusory psychological creations must end.

No one ever comes to the "subject" with right intent, except the individual who has had a total crisis in his life. Only the individual who through actual living experiences has been awakened to the emptiness, uselessness and futility of his activities, and the activities of others, as a means of fulfilling life, can come to the "subject" with real intent. There must have been an inner shock, deep anguish, and a dead end inside, in which there is a complete rejection (not denunciation) of the objectives that he has been pursuing; also an understanding of the valuelessness of these objective as an adequate answer to life. These objectives are a continuous round of similarly repeated experiences in sensation. It is an awakening to the fact that all there has ever been in one's life are various forms of sensation, and that if something else doesn't take place in one, that's all there ever will be. There has to be the shock of realization that as you now live, all that life has been for you, is nothing more than sensation; that this sensation is the only actual reason you have found for living. At this point you may know nothing more. But you cannot accept sensation as the ultimate fulfillment of man. You realize that it is untenable, preposterous and ridiculous. Then in you a new process in consciousness has been started. This unsought, effortless awakening and fulfillment in self-knowledge, gives birth to real intent. It may be that all you can say is, "If there is something real, more intrinsic than fleeting sensation to living, then it must be understood." Then you are open; the self and its sensations are secondary. They will cease to be the motivation of your life. New intent, interest and endeavor will be the primary motivation, direction and activity of your life. For the first time the illusory sensory fulfillment of fame, honor, power, property, position, place, idealistic manmade virtue, success, victory, sex, pride of person, family, country, ability, talent, possessions and so on, will have lost their former significance and grasp on you. Self-achievement will not be the primary motivation of your life, hence the intellect will allow denudement. You will be able to meet, discern and understand "what is" in your life. You will know the true significance of living.

How is it possible to do anything without intent? How can there be adequate action unless intent is known? And how can intent be real unless it is outside the field of sensation, unless man wakes up to the illusory values of sensation and becomes free of them? Nothing is possible for man unless there is real intent.

Without it, he can never move from his present position. He may try, but all his efforts will be more of the old intent, sensation.

So, through the awakening to and the understanding of the false elements of the duality process in ourselves, a new responsibility comes into being. With the significance of new responsibility, the need for right relationship is born.

Out of this new responsibility comes new motivation, response and direction in living. That is, new intent and aim are born, a vital need to know and be "what is." Clarity of endeavor is seen to be the need to be constantly alert and responsive to fact. Vital interest and enthusiasm is the serious giving of one's self totally to understanding "what is," reality. Dedication is born of fact, of need. And when it is experienced and used, you will be able to go into self-knowledge without desire, without an objective, without an end in view. The cornerstone is simplicity, which makes possible that nonresistant state in which man is open for self-approach, self-observation and self-knowledge. He is free of constant self-protective resistances and psychological complexities.

CHAPTER 37

Needs

*So when man becomes conscious of his psychological thoughts
and emotions on all levels, he discerns that they are only desire
in constant reaction, the constant desire of self-satisfaction.
When he becomes conscious that it is desire that manifests
as consciousness, whether it be greed, gossip, cruelty, vanity,
pride, deceit, or any one of a thousand other negative qualities,
when he perceives and knows he is what consciousness is, it is a
recognition of fact, a recognition of need.*

You need to become aware of your many needs. You need to become aware of the fact that you are caught in self-consciousness, so that you may become totally alert to it. You need to realize that you are not simple, but complex. You are not sensitive but intensified self-consciousness; that you are not spontaneously aware but are studiously self-centered and your action is constantly self-protective stemming from uncertainty and insecurity.

You need to awaken to the fact that you have been trying to achieve personal results through the use of knowledge about the self, not self-knowledge; hence you have developed psychological self-consciousness. You need to realize that you are a self-obstructive, closed process, through which the development of self-consciousness increased, and so getting caught in it was inevitable.

You need to recognize the fact that you always meet every experience as a self-achieving process for you cannot and do not meet experiences otherwise.

You need to realize that as you are, you cannot go beyond, for the intellect cannot conceive of anything beyond its acquired concepts. You need to realize that it will be necessary to start anew, that you make a thorough study of the primary obstruction to right thinking and feeling, namely, the problem of desire and its self-formulated psychological process, the "duality process." You need to realize that the self-achieving dualistic process of thinking and feeling is valueless in the solution of problems in relationship. You need to awaken to the futility and uselessness of this desire process, for its constant and continuous manifestation is nothing more than an endless series of conflicts, confusion and suffering. You need to realize that nothing in you ever changes for your good when you use the dual process; that with this dualistic process you always meet the problems of life in the same manner, achieve the same ends and everything remains the same.

You need to recognize that what you consider to be change is nothing more than an intensification of the "I." Nothing basically has changed. You are the same, a security seeking process.

You need to realize that it will be most difficult not to continue this habitual self-expansive process.

You need to awaken to the fact that you have not been moving solely from a study of the duality process for the purpose of becoming familiar with its substance. Instead, from the beginning, you have been applying to yourself all that you have heard or read. That is, you must recognize that you have been moving first with desire and concern for your own thoughts, feelings and actions, from the initial contact with the subject.

You must realize you have very little of your own and when you do react, you will use that which belongs for the most part to others. You must awaken to the fact you put the emphasis for conflict on the other person or on the outside situation, thereby moving away from center, yourself, your thoughts, the source of your conflict. You need to realize the pointing out of the faults of others is the manifestation of ignorance.

You must face the fact that your concern is first for yourself.

You need to awaken to the fact that you cannot change another, nor is their change your concern. It is not, nor can it ever be, your job to try and change another, for that responsibility is entirely theirs.

You need to accept the use of relationship as a mirror in which you, not the other, may be revealed, and not as a device for obtaining self-satisfaction.

You need to awaken to the fact that you have been using knowledge of the self as a mechanism to avoid and escape from "what is" in yourselves.

You need to understand that post-event discussions and commentaries are mostly intellectual escapes and avail nothing real, and that they destroy the intrinsic value of the moment. You need to realize that if you fail to understand and act in the moment, the possibility of understanding the content of that moment is lost forever, and all attempts to recall it are useless, and all comments about it are valueless.

You need to awaken to the fact that whatever the "I" does intensifies your state and creates greater emotional instability and uncertainty; that a continued sense of failure and guilt prevail; that irritation, resentment and anger are always on the threshold of consciousness. That fear is your constant companion, causing you to blame all else, but yourself, for your predicament. Fear forces you to grasp at or create anything that will take you away from yourself.

You need to realize that psychology cannot solve the psychological problems of the mind, for their solutions lie outside the scope of the mind, outside the psychological thinking process.

You need to awaken to the futility and uselessness of continuing the self-achieving process, for its constant and continuous manifestation brings only an endless series of conflicts, confusion and suffering.

You need to realize that it will be necessary to start anew, that you need to make a thorough study of the primary essential, the problem of desire, and its self-created psychological mechanism, the "duality process." You must understand its origin, components, processes, manifestations and be these fictitious significances in consciousness. This process must be thoroughly understood before you again become concerned with your own thoughts, feelings and actions. If this is done, there can be established an adequate means, awareness without identification, whereby, without effort, you will be confronted with what you are, and through which it will be possible to experience self-knowledge and spontaneous action. It will be possible to establish within, a new faculty through which you will be accurately and factually revealed.

It is possible for one to be free of the self-achieving, self-protective process; it is possible to go beyond the use of the intellect, but one must realize it will be an extremely difficult task, for as of now you are totally this type of consciousness, and to use any of its components or processes is to deter yourself. You must eventually meet the problems and experiences of life in a manner heretofore unknown. To do this, you must first perceive all that prevents and obstructs understanding, and fulfill that which is required and needed to meet life as a whole, and not as a particular, not as a self-centered being, one who sets himself apart from everything. We must realize, acknowledge and accept the fact that as we are, we cannot do anything about the "new," about "regeneration." Nor do we know how to be free of the "old" psychological desires, that which we are. Yet something must be done. From the psychological point of view, this seems impossible. How can you go into anything without an end in view, without desire and purpose being present? The very going implies desire and purpose, or why go? You will find the answer in the differentiation between desire and need, fact. You have experiences in both desire and need, but usually you do not differentiate between them, because you do not understand need for what it is, or what it indicates, nor do you understand the significance of psychological desire, want. You use these words interchangeably, considering them to have similar meaning. Most of your needs have been converted into psychological wants, desires. To these you have added a host of other artificial desires, filling your consciousness with an unending stream of psychological wants, all of which you call needs. Desire and purpose are born of conditioning and all such motivations are only reactions of conditioning. Man's desire is self-engendered for the fulfillment of the self in satisfactions.

Desire and purpose are the same thing, for purpose is only another form of desire. In psychological desire, there is always a self-protective purpose. Desire is extraneous to need.

Need, fact, exists of itself and cannot be artificially created. It always remains what it is, its nature cannot be induced or changed. In it there is no desire, for need indicates its own designation and fulfillment. Man, in his recognition of need, responds to it, and becomes its designation and action. In this there is no psychological desire or purpose, just intelligent response to the factual, in keeping with the level of the need. Hence when man is response as need, that is when he is fact as consciousness, he is not moving from desire nor does he have an end in view. For example, on the physical level, man becomes conscious he is hungry. It is recognition of fact, of need, and his initial response to this alertment, which came of its own, from a source independent of psychological mind, which brings with it all elements necessary for understanding its significance and fulfillment without the presence of desire. That is, the motivation, means and end are known, and this brings an action in keeping with the revealed need. All inner functions based on real need (not desires) manifest identically the same, and in keeping with all levels of consciousness. To live through need, fact, is the way of understanding. For the man who knows all his needs, needs nothing else.

So when man becomes conscious of his psychological thoughts and emotions on all levels, he discerns that they are only desire in constant reaction, the constant desire of self-satisfaction. When he becomes conscious that it is desire that manifests as consciousness, whether it be greed, gossip, cruelty, vanity, pride, deceit, or any one of a thousand other negative qualities, when he perceives and knows he is what consciousness is, it is a recognition of fact, a recognition of need. His initial response to this awakening, this alertment, is an intelligent response to need. All the elements essential for understanding its significance and the action required in keeping with need are known; the motivation, means and the end are known. Action then follows in keeping with fact, with need.

The words fact or need used here are synonymous in significance. Need is the functional essence of fact. Fact and need are objective in essence and not subjective. They denote and signify non-manmade, preestablished, unchangeable objective designations, which are correlated to every expression of life. Through them the meaning and function of each will be revealed. Our innate purpose is to be a channel through which these factual designations, extrinsic and intrinsic facts, creative manifestations, may find expression. It is essential to know that not we, but something not of us, can function through us that will determine what is real, actual and what should be.

Intrinsic fact reveals the true meaning and nature of physical facts; it also reveals the meaning and nature of all manmade psychological facts. Intrinsic fact reveals all psychological thoughts and psycho-emotional feeling reactions through which man at present lives and has his being; it reveals his artificially created self, personality and its self-centered, self-protective way of life and what should be done about it. Objective fact, intrinsic need, reveals and designates the true nature of man's relationship to man, to all things and to himself. It is the source of true self-knowledge.

We are not concerned with intrinsic fact for the purpose of gaining knowledge or for the purpose of its possession and use on our behalf. On the physical level, our concern is to function in keeping with physical need, physical facts. On the physiological level to function in keeping with physiological facts, to fulfill the needs indicated, to use the senses for what they were intended, and not for psychological wants. On the psychological level to face the falsity of self-engendered artificial "facts," and be free of them, and on the intrinsic level, the human spiritual level, to be a channel through which these facts may express their creative action. For us, fact is need, the essential in the now. It has always existed, exists in the present and will continue to exist. It can be experienced on all levels, but cannot be given or translated to another. Fact does not demand the thought process and can be contacted only when psychological thought and feeling have ceased. Fact is of another dimension and needs no confirmation. It needs no psychological interpretation, for it signifies its meaning without fail. It is directness, action, understanding. It is the whole. Intrinsic fact is the means through which man may fulfill the purpose of his being, a channel for the expression of creative action, and this is his highest responsibility. And when man has become responsible to life, to God, he will then be responsible to others, to all things and to himself.

CHAPTER 38

Creativeness

Creativeness is quite a different state of being. It is a state in which the self is absent, in which the mind is no longer a focus of your experiences, your ambitions, your pursuits and your desires. Creativeness is not a continuous state. It is new from moment to moment.

What do we mean by creativeness? Is it creative to invent the atomic bomb, to discover a more effective way of killing people? Is it creative to have a capacity, a gift? Is it creative to speak very cleverly, to write very intelligent books, to solve problems? Is it creative to discover the process of nature, the hidden process of life? Are any of these a state of creativeness? Or, is creativeness something entirely different from created self-expression? I may have the capacity to translate into marble a certain vision, a certain feeling; or, being a scientist, I may be able to discover something new, according to my tendencies and capacities. But is that creativeness? Is the expression of a feeling, the making of a discovery, the writing of a book or poem, the painting of a picture—are any of these necessarily creative? Or, is creativeness something utterly different, which is not dependent on self-expression? To us, self-expression seems to matter so enormously—to be able to say something in words, in a picture, in a poem, to be able to concentrate on the discovery of a particular scientific fact—is that a process of creation? Or, is creation something that is not of the mind at all? After all, when the mind demands, it will find an answer; but is its answer the creative answer?

You think that to have a technique, to be able to draw, to write a poem or an article, to fulfill yourself in one form or another, is to be creative. That is not creativeness: that is self-expression, satisfying a certain urge through technique. To most of you, creativeness is a process of self-expression, it is the power to do something "creative." You consider that self-expression is far more important than to be free. You want and crave for expression because it gives you a sense of fulfillment, a sense of importance, achievement. It gives you the feeling of being somebody, of being socially useful. All this feeds your vanity in many ways, and so destroys the state of creativeness.

Surely, your difficulty is that most of you have lost your sense of creativeness. To be creative does not mean that you must paint pictures or write poems and become famous. That is not creativeness—it is merely the capacity to express an idea, which the public applauds or disregards. Capacity and creativeness should not be confused. Capacity is not creativeness. Creativeness is not the building of huge industries, organizations or the construction of massive structures and edifices, for these are but forms of self-expression.

Most of you are not creative. You are repetitive machines, mere phonograph records playing over and over again certain experiences, certain conclusions and memories, either your own or those of another. Such repetition is not creative being—but it is what you want, because you want to be inwardly secure. You are constantly seeking methods and means for this security by self-expression, or you create authority, the worship of another.

Creativeness is quite a different state of being. It is a state in which the self is absent, in which the mind is no longer a focus of your experiences, your ambitions, your pursuits and your desires. Creativeness is not a continuous state. It is new from moment to moment. It is movement in which there is no "me" and "mine," in which the thought is not focused on any particular experience, ambition, achievement, purpose or motive. It is only when the self is not, that there is that spontaneous tranquility of mind in which alone there can be a state of creativeness.

That state cannot be conceived or imagined. It cannot be formulated or copied. It cannot be attained through any discipline, any method, any technique. On the contrary, it comes into being only through understanding the total process of yourself. Self-expression is not creativeness; to be truly creative, you must understand the process of the self and be free from it.

The understanding of yourself is not a result, a culmination; it is seeing yourself from moment to moment in the mirror of relationship—your relationship to property, to things, to people and to ideas. But you find it difficult to be alert, to be aware. You prefer to dull your mind by following a method, by accepting authorities, superstitions and gratifying theories; so your mind becomes weary, exhausted and insensitive. Such a mind cannot be in a state of creativeness. The state of creativeness—transformation—comes only when the self, which is the process of recognition and accumulation, ceases to be. And consciousness, as the "me," is the center of recognition, and recognition is the memory of accumulated experiences. But you are afraid to be nothing. You want to *be* something. The little man wants to be a big man, the non-virtuous want to be virtuous, the weak and obscure crave power, position and authority; the lonely crave affection, the powerful want to dominate and control. This is the incessant activity of the mind. Such a mind cannot be quiet and therefore can never be in the state of creativeness.

What is preventing you from being creative? Technique. You always know what to do; you have the means. All your education is a process of learning techniques, which means a process of imitation, a process of copying. Knowledge is imitation, copy; and isn't that one of the major burdens that prevents you from meeting things anew? Is not authority in any form, spiritual or mundane, external or inward, an impediment to creative understanding? And why do you have authorities? Because, without authority you are lost. You must have some anchor, and that very authority, which obviously means imitation, destroys creative newness.

Truth is a state of creativeness. It cannot be realized through imitation, through copying, through authority, through compulsion.

Must one not be free from authority, from all sense of imitation and copying? You will say, "No, we must look to authority in order to be free; we must begin with imitation in order ultimately to arrive at freedom." But if you take the wrong means, can you come to the right end? If the end is freedom, must not the beginning also be free? If you use a wrong means, obviously the end must be equally wrong; and if you have no freedom at the beginning, you will have no freedom at the end. If, at the beginning, your mind is controlled, shaped, disciplined, molded according to some authority or someone you admire, obviously it will still be encompassed, held in a frame, at the end. Such a mind can never be in a state of creativeness. So, in the beginning is the end; the end and the means are the same.

If you are to understand creativeness, the beginning matters enormously, which means understanding all those things that impede the mind and prevent its freedom. Freedom comes only when you understand your desire to be secure. It is the desire to be secure that creates authority, that creates discipline, the pattern of imitation, the pursuit of the ideal, the whole process of conformity. The loftier the ideal, the nobler, the holier, the more creative you think it is. But it is still a pattern; and a mind caught in a pattern is not capable of being creative. But seeing that the mind is caught in a pattern, merely to reject it, as a reaction, is not freedom either. But in understanding *why* the mind creates a pattern and holds on to it, *why* the mind is caught in technique, in the addiction to knowledge, *why* the mind always moves from the known to the known, from security to security, from imitation to imitation—in direct understanding of that, there is freedom from the desire for security and therefore from fear. As long as there is a center of the "me," from which there is action and reaction, denial and acceptance, there must be a process of imitation and copy. As long as you are mere repeaters, reading books, quoting authorities, pursuing ideals, conforming to a formula or to a dogma, holding on to a particular religion or joining new cults, seeking new teachers—as long as that process exists there can be no freedom. So creativeness comes only when the mind is free from all imitation, from all experience. The mind is free when there is no "me" that is experiencing. And that center in the mind disappears when the whole process of desire is understood.

We are the result of society, we are the depositories of society. We either conform to society, or break away from society. The breaking away from society depends upon our background, our conditioning; therefore, our breaking away from society does not indicate that we are free—it may be merely the reaction of our conditioning. So, a man who is creative merely in the accepted sense of the word may be dangerous, disruptive, if he is not transformed in any fundamental way. Only then can he help in the transformation of the respectable, exploiting society, which is ours.

Society is the outcome of your own projections, of your own intentions. You are not separate from society. The man who goes against society is not necessarily a revolutionary. Is it not important to understand what we mean by revolution? A revolution based on a belief, on a dogma, on knowledge, is no revolution at all; it is merely a modified continuation of the old. A reaction of the background against the conditioning influence of society is an escape, it is not a revolution.

Is revolution a matter of technique? A political revolution, a sociological revolution may need a certain technique because you can pursue a certain ideology to produce a certain result—whether it is the communist ideology or the fascist, or the capitalist, you must learn a technique to produce a result; but is that a fundamental revolution? A fundamental revolution in yourself is necessary if you are to be in a state of creativeness. Will a technique produce that true revolution? There must be a radical, fundamental, sociological revolution. Your whole being has to be transformed. For this to happen there must be individuals, you and me, who understand the problem, and who in themselves are in a state of revolution. Then their action upon society is revolutionary. They are not merely learning a technique of revolution. They themselves are in revolution, a state of true creativeness.

Is it not more important, more essential, that you be in a creative state of revolution, rather than trying to find a technique of revolution? Why aren't you revolutionary? Why isn't there a new process of life in you? Why are you not truly creative? Why do you not have in you a new way of looking at life, a flame, a tremendous discontent? Why? Because a person who is completely discontented, not merely discontented with certain things, but inherently discontented, needs have no technique to be revolutionary. He is revolutionary. What is important is not the technique, but to be revolutionary, to awaken to the importance of complete transformation. For without transformation, you will not be creative. And when you are transformed, then you will be able to act, then there is the constant flow of newness, creativeness, which is the true revolution.

Surely, then, the important thing is to discover what it is to be creative. Creativeness can be discovered and understood, the truth of it seen only when you understand the total process of yourself. The importance of inward revolution, of psychological transformation, is far greater than outer revolution. The outer revolution is merely change, which is modified continuity. But inner revolution has no resting place, there is no stopping, it is constantly renewing itself. That is what we need at this present time—people who are completely discontented and therefore ready to perceive the truth of things. A person who is complacent, who is satisfied with money, with position, with an idea, with sensation, can never see truth. Only the person who is discontented, who is investigating, who is asking, questioning, looking can discover truth. Such a person is a revolution himself and therefore is revolutionary in his relationships. Therefore, in his world, which is his relationship with people—he begins to transform. Then he affects the world within his own relationships. So, merely to look for a technique, or to inquire what is another's technique for the new revolution, is beside the point. You miss the importance of being revolutionary in yourself.

There can be revolution, the inner, continuous renewal, creativeness, only when you understand yourself to have that knowledge of yourself at whatever level can only be learned in relationship. And as relationship is often painful, is constantly in motion, you want to escape from it and find a reality outside relationship. There is no reality outside relationship. When you understand relationship, then that very understanding is reality. You have to be extraordinarily alert, awake, all the time watching, open to every challenge and to every suggestion and hint. That demands a certain alertness of mind and heart; but most of you are asleep, most of you, though you may be young, already have one foot in the grave. You think in terms of achievement, you think in terms of gain. You are never living; you are always concerned with the end; you are end seekers, not moving with life. Therefore you are never revolutionary, never creative. If you are concerned directly with life, with living and not with the idea about living, then you cannot help but be a revolution in yourself. You will be a revolution, because you are meeting life directly, not through the screen of words, prejudice, intentions and ends.

The man who meets life directly is a man who is in a state of discontent; and you must be in a state of discontent to find reality, to find creativeness, inner revolution. It is creativeness that releases, that frees the mind from its illusions. If you can understand this whole process of conflict, this striving after attainment, which brings in your life such contradiction, such sorrow and pain, then you will see that the mind becomes very quiet, without any striving; and when the mind is silent, free of the anxieties and demands of the self, only then is there a possibility of creative being. When every movement of psychological thought is understood and therefore comes to an end, only then is there creativeness.

When the mind is quiet, there comes that creative something, which is creation itself. It will find its own expression. When there is the creative urge, it will find its own technique, or its own means of expression. If you are painter, you will paint. If you are a writer, you will write. It is that creative understanding that is vital, that gives grace, that gives happiness.

So, reality, or God, or creativeness, or what you will is something that cannot come through a technique, through a means, through long, determined practice and discipline. It is not a course laid out with a known end. You must enter the unchartered seas. There must be aloneness. Aloneness implies no means. You are not alone when you have a means, a method, a technique. There must be complete nakedness, emptiness of all these accumulated practices, hopes, pleasures, desires for security, which are all consistently maintaining a means, a method, a technique. Then only is there the other, and then the problem is solved. A man who is dying from moment to moment, and therefore renewing from moment to moment, is not separate from life; he is life.

CHAPTER 39

Love

*There is only one love. Compassion, forgiveness, generosity and
kindness cannot exist if there is no love. Without love,
all virtues become cruel and destructive.*

You must understand your present attitude toward love to understand what true love is. If you really think about it, you will see that your love is now based on possessiveness. You will see that your laws, ethics and morals are founded on this desire to hold and control.

You depend on sensation for the continuance of so-called love, and when that gratification is withheld, you try to find it with another. So what you are seeking most often is satisfaction of desire in your human relationships. Relationship is now based on your psychological satisfaction, happiness and well-being.

The will of desire ever seeks to make love a mechanical habit, or tries to control it through moral laws, through compulsion. There is a constant battle in the mind, with its will for satisfaction, to control, dominate love.

When you love another, your passions, your possessive love and jealousy are aroused. You find sorrow and conflict in this relationship, and because you cannot resolve this ache, you try to dominate, control the other or you run away from the ache.

Where there is love, there is no consciousness of relationship. It is only in a state of resistance that there can be this consciousness of relationship, which is merely adjustment between opposing conflicts. Where there is the possibility of pain, where there is the possibility of suffering in love, it is not love, it is merely a subtle form of possessiveness, of acquisitiveness.

If you love, really love someone there is no possibility of giving pain when you do something which you think is right. It is only when you want that person to do what you desire or he wants you to do what he desires that there is pain. That is, you like to be possessed, you feel safe, secure, comfortable. So both of you struggle for comfort, for encouragement, from and through the other, and therefore any action that does not bring satisfaction naturally creates disturbance, pain, suffering. One individual is always suppressing what he really feels in order to adjust himself to the other. This constant suppression, brought on by so-called love, destroys the two individuals. In that love, there is no freedom; it is merely subtle bondage. In this kind of relationship it is only when you feel very desperate that you do something, sometimes cunningly and subtly, but you do it. There is always this urge to do, to act independently. But it is caught in bondage. To love is to be free—both parties free.

When in human relationships there is friction, pain, you try to idealize love and call it cosmic, universal, God. This is but an escape from reality. You hope to love man through the love of God, but if you do not know how to love man how can you love reality, God? To love man *is* to love reality. But you find that to love another is painful. So many complex problems are involved in a relationship, you think it is easier and more satisfying to love an ideal, which is an intellectual emotionalism, not love. Because you do not know how to love human beings, you love masters, ideals, God, "creative" work, business, etc. If you cannot love another without possessiveness, without conflict and pain, with which we are all so familiar, if you don't understand this, how can you hope to understand and love something else, especially when in this something there is a great possibility of self-deception? Where is love to begin—with God, and masters, and ideals of achievement, or with human beings?

How can there be love when you have your individual prejudices, racial antagonisms, national hatreds, and economic conflicts? How can you love another when you are mainly concerned with your own security, with your own growth, with your own well-being? This so-called love of ideals, masters, God, is romantic and false. The worship of masters, ideals, is idolatry and destructive of understanding and love.

Do not divide love artificially as the love of God and the love of man. There is only one love. Compassion, forgiveness, generosity and kindness cannot exist if there is no love. Without love, all virtues become cruel and destructive.

We all have the capacity for deep and inclusive love, but through conflict and false relationship, sensation and habit, we destroy its beauty. Through possessiveness with its many cruelties, through all the ugliness of reciprocal exploitation, we slowly extinguish the flame of love. There cannot be love, creative intelligence, so long as there is fear and possessiveness in any form. How can there be deep love when there is this desire to possess, to hold? When the mind is free of possessiveness, there is love.

If you base your understanding merely on reason, then in it there is isolation, pride, a lack of love. If you base your understanding merely on emotion, then in it there is no depth, no love, there is only sentimentality, which soon evaporates.

Since your relationship is based on possessive love, you have to become aware in yourself of its birth, its causes, its action. In becoming deeply aware of the process of possessiveness, with its violence, its fears, its action, there comes an understanding that is whole. To love without fear, without possessiveness, demands an intense awareness and understanding, which can only be realized in human relationship. When thought is freed from craving and possessiveness, then only can there be the love of the whole. When you face this problem deeply, there is a new awakening, a state which is love. If the mind is alert without the duality of the observer and the observed, if mind can know itself as it is, without denial, assertion, acceptance or resignation, then out of that very actuality there comes love, creative intelligence.

You can know yourself only when you love completely. You cannot be yourself when love is dependent. It is not love when it is merely self-gratification, though it may be mutual. It is not love when there is a withholding; it is not love when it is merely a means to an end, when it is merely sensation. You cannot be yourself when love is based on fear; it is then fear, not love, that is expressing itself in many ways, though you may cover it up by calling it love.

To be utterly yourself, integral in your whole being is to be unconditioned. Only in unconditioned freedom is there truth, love.

So what is it to be oneself? And can you be yourself at all times? You can be yourself at all times if you are doing something that you really love, if you love completely. When you are doing something that you cannot help doing with your whole being, you are being yourself. Or when you love another completely, in that state you are yourself, without any fear, without any hindrance. In these two states, you are completely yourself. So you have to find out what it is you love to do. What is it that with your whole being you love to do?

Where there is love, true love, there is no question of sin, of legality or illegality. But unless you really think about this, unless you make a real effort not to misunderstand what is being said, it will lead to confusion.

You cannot know love through the description of another. You know love only when you have experienced it yourself.

What love is, what compassion is, you yourself will know when your mind and heart are free from the limitation of egotism, self-consciousness; then you will know without asking, without discussion.

Only when desire ceases of its own spontaneous accord, not through compulsion or promise of reward, is there a renewal, a rebirth of one's whole being. Responsibility in relationship, then, is not based on satisfaction, but on understanding and love.

CHAPTER 40

Awareness

To be free you must be fully self-conscious, and through that flame of awareness, through that intensity of aloneness, you will come to the realization of that life, which is not inclusiveness nor an exclusiveness, in which there is no distinction and therefore no resistance. Where that understanding exists, there is true individuality, true aloneness—not the aloneness of escape into solitude, but the aloneness that is born of the full comprehension of the experiences of life.

We have relied on the intellect to show us a way out of our complexity. So far we have used the mind, the intellect, the thinking process to help us investigate our problems, and by this process are hoping to find a solution. But the more cunning, the more subtle the intellect, the more apt our thinking, the greater the variety of systems, of theories, of ideas, the further we are from the solution of our problem.

By thinking over a psychological problem, have you resolved it? Any kind of problem—economic, social, religious—has it ever been really solved by thinking? In your daily life, the more you think about a problem, the more complex, the more irresolute, the more uncertain it becomes. You may, in thinking out certain facets of the problem, see more clearly another's point of view. You may think you have solved the problem when adjustments in the problem seem to ease a particular situation or when the problem seems to drop away, but this is only a superficial solution of the problem. It will arise again, and again, or another problem will take its place. Thought cannot see the completeness and fullness of the problem. It can only see partially. It can only have ideas about the problem. Ideas do not solve any human problem; they never have and never will. They are not the solution.

What is thinking? When we say, "I think," what do we mean by thinking? When are we conscious of this process of thinking? Surely we are aware of it when there is a problem, when we are challenged, when we are asked a question, when there is friction. We are aware of it as a self-conscious process.

Thinking is a reaction. If I ask you a question, to that you respond. You respond according to your memory, to your prejudices, to your upbringing, to the climate, to the whole background of your conditioning. And according to that reply, you think. If you are a Christian, a Hindu, a communist, or what you will, it is that background that responds. So it is this conditioning that obviously creates the problem. And the center of this background is the "me," the "I," in the process of action. So long as that background is not understood, so long as that thought process, that self, which creates the problem, is not understood and put an end to, you are bound to have conflict, within and without, in thought, in emotion, in action.

No solution of any kind, however clever, however well-thought-out, can ever put an end to that conflict between the "me" and "you." Thought, unless it is in the laboratory or on the drawing board, is always protecting, self-perpetuating, conditioned. Its activity is self-centered. And can such thought ever resolve any of the problems that thought itself created? Can the mind, which has created the problems, resolve those things that it has itself brought forth? That is, can mind, thought, get rid of itself, while using itself? The mind is not the solution; the way of psychological thought is not the way out of our difficulty. And realizing this, being aware of how thought springs up and from what source, we ask, can psychological thought ever come to an end? Can the self ever come to an end?

It is possible for thought to be brought to an end, but there must be an awareness, which is not thought. To be aware, without condemnation or justification, of the activities of the self, just to be aware is sufficient. That is, we can understand the self, not by analyzing, but by seeing the self as it is, being aware of it as a fact and not as a theory. Not seeking to dissolve the self in order to achieve a result, but seeing the activity of the self, the "me," constantly in action. If we can look at it without any moment to destroy or discourage, then it is possible to be free of the "me," the "I." And if, in each of us, the center of the me is nonexistent, with its desire for power, position, authority, continence, self-preservation, surely our psychological thought and thinking will come to an end.

You are not going to be aware by merely reading these pages. It is as a fire, which must be built, and you must build it. You must begin, however little, to be aware, and this you can do when you talk, when you laugh, when you come into contact with people, or when you are still. This awareness becomes a flame, and this flame consumes all fear. The mind must reveal itself spontaneously to itself. And this is not given only to a few, nor is it an impossibility.

But if you are aware in order to find out how to resolve your problem, in order to transform it, in order to produce a result, then it is still within the field of the self, the "me." So long as you are seeking a result, whether through analysis, through awareness, through constant examination of every thought, which is within the field of the "me," of the "I," of the ego, it will not be possible to bring the thinking process to an end.

To understand yourself profoundly, you need balance. This is, you cannot abandon the world, hoping to understand yourself, or be so entangled in the world that there is no time to comprehend yourself. There must be balance, neither renunciation nor acquiescence. This demands alertness and deep awareness. You must learn to observe your actions, thoughts, feelings, ideals, beliefs, silently without judgment, without interpreting them, so as to be able to discern their true significance. You must first be cognizant of your own ideals, pursuits, wants, without accepting or condemning them as right or wrong. At present you cannot discern what is true and what is false, what is lasting and what is transient, because the mind is so crippled with its own self-created wants, ideals and escapes. It is incapable of true perception. So you must learn to be a silent and balanced observer of your limitations and frictions.

The only actuality, the only reality that you can fully comprehend, is this confusion, this misery, this conflict; but to escape from this is to create illusion. If you escape from actuality, you will depend on illusions, hopes, longings, which have no reality. Not living in actuality must inevitably lead to illusion, though this illusion may have assumed a reality through time and tradition. Actuality is that which you experience yourself. It has nothing to do with faith or with the rejection of that which is imperceptible to the senses. You cannot experience a theory, an explanation. You can discover actuality only when you have understood and dissolved the process of ignorance.

To discover reality, to discover your true substance, you must be free from fear. First, from the fear of salvation, because no one is going to save you except yourself. Do not look for salvation from the outside in any form, or you will create new conventions instead of the old. What you have to create is the man who is certain of his salvation in himself, who is strong, certain of his purpose and not looking for external comfort, external authority, external encouragement. No erection of churches, creation of gods and images, no prayers, no worship, no ceremonies, are going to give you that inner understanding and tranquility. You must be free from ancient gods and modern gods; free from the fear of punishment and the enticement of reward; free from the fear of loss and gain; free from the fear of loneliness and longing for companionship; free from the fear of convention; free from the fear of not expressing yourself; free of love and hate, desire, ambition, jealousy, envy, life and death—you must be free of all that, in order to discover what remains.

You can attain freedom wherever you are, but that means that you must have the strength of a genius. For a genius, after all, is a person who is not held back by his circumstances, who is beyond his circle. So if a person thinks that here or elsewhere he can develop his unique perfection, before he leaves this or any other place, before finally deciding, let him understand that wherever he is, if he is not strong enough, his circumstances will drown him; that wherever he is, he can fulfill understanding and live creatively.

True search begins only when there is a release from those reactions that are the result of division. Without the understanding of life's wholeness the search for truth and happiness must lead to illusion. Wanting indicates an emptiness, a trying to become something, whereas true search leads to deep comprehension. Man's present purpose is his search for security, certainty and continuity. When you understand the significance of your existence, of the process of ignorance and action, you will see that what you call purpose has no significance. The mere search for the purpose of life covers up, detracts from the comprehension of oneself.

True search requires a very quiet mind, a very still mind, so that the mind can look at the problem without interposing ideas, theories, without any distraction. And this is only possible when the process of psychological thinking—which has its source in the me, the self, in the background of tradition, conditioning, of prejudices; of hope, of despair—has come to an end. Then it will be possible to look at the problem comprehensively, wholly. Then only can it be solved, when you look at it as a whole, not in compartments, not divided. For a mind that is not distracted by its own thought, a mind that is open, a mind that is very quiet, can look at the problem directly and simply. And it is this capacity to look without distraction at your problems that is the solution.

Such a mind is not a result, it is not an end product of a practice, of meditation, of control. It comes into being through no form of discipline, compulsion or sublimation, without any effort of the me, of thought; it comes into being when I understand the whole thinking process—when I can see a fact without any distraction. In that state of tranquility of a mind that is really still, there is love. And it is love alone that solves all your problems.

So, seeing this problem, this complex problem of living, and being aware of the process of your own thinking, realizing that it leads nowhere and bringing it to an end—when you deeply realize and fulfill that, then there is a state of intelligence, which is not individual or collective. So, the problem of relationship of the individual to society, of the individual to the community, of the individual to reality ceases; because there is only intelligence, which is neither personal nor impersonal. Where there is intelligence functioning, there is no consciousness of individuality. Intelligence is free of the individual and the collective. Intelligence is unique; it cannot be divided into yours and mine; it is neither superior nor inferior. Intelligence has no concern with the conception of security. It arranges the well-being of the whole, and not merely the particular. It is creative intuition, love, and its action is true harmony.

So, when the thinking process has ended, when you don't want to be anything, but live completely in a day, in the richness of a single day, you will know what simplicity, masterhood or liberation is. For when man begins to understand both inner and outer environment, sees its full worth, then he is master of his actions, then he is intelligent and therefore no matter what the condition, he will function intelligently. That is, to be free you must be fully self-conscious, and through that flame of awareness, through that intensity of aloneness, you will come to the realization of that life, which is not inclusiveness nor an exclusiveness, in which there is no distinction and therefore no resistance.

Where that understanding exists, there is true individuality, true aloneness—not the aloneness of escape into solitude, but the aloneness that is born of the full comprehension of the experiences of life.

CHAPTER 41

The Art of Living

Living is the harmonious action of thought, emotion and work; when these are in contradiction with each other, then there is suffering, conflict, disharmony. To love and work harmoniously, completely, there must be the highest intelligence. This state is without fear, without exploitation and without seeking a reward.

Nature contains life, that is, everything in manifestation contains life in itself. The whole destiny and function of this life force, nature, is to create the self-conscious individual, who knows he is an entity in himself, conscious and separate. The life force in nature, through its self-development becomes self-conscious in the awakened, concentrated individual. When the life in nature develops and becomes focused in the individual, then nature has fulfilled itself.

Civilization is not an achievement. It is a constant movement. The real function of civilization should be to allow man to develop himself freely, and to free himself from the sense of the self. The present form of civilization does the opposite, for it restricts, dominates, controls and retards man. Civilizations reach a certain height, exist for a time, and then decline because in them there is no fulfillment for man, but only constant imitation of a pattern. There is completeness, fulfillment, only when mind and heart are part of this constant movement, of search. Civilizations should not search for a permanency, a certainty; then living would not be a series of culminations, but a continual movement, a fulfillment in search.

If society is merely attempting to reach an ideal, society will soon decay. If civilization is merely an achievement of individuals collected as a group, it is already in the process of decay. But if society, civilization, is the outcome of a constant movement, an open search, then it will endure.

Examine our structure of thought, emotion, our whole civilization. You will see that it is a process of conformity. When we suffer, our immediate reaction is a desire for relief, for consolation. We accept the theories and conclusions, the imaginings offered by the few, without finding out the cause of suffering. We are momentarily satisfied, and so we do not find out profoundly for ourselves that the cause of our suffering is; we stop the search.

Many civilizations have come and gone. Those of the present are in the process of decay. Decadence is observed everywhere. Man today is blindly and hurriedly preparing for total annihilation.

We are concerned with living, and living implies not only shelter, food, clothing and work, but also love and thought. We cannot understand the full significance of living if we deal separately, singly, with the problem of work, of love, of thought. They are interrelated and inseparable. They must be understood comprehensively, as a whole. The people who are comfortably settled in life are following the traditional pattern or system, and they try to separate work from living. They hope to overcome the conflict that arises from this division by considering each problem separately.

Living is the harmonious action of thought, emotion and work; when these are in contradiction with each other, then there is suffering, conflict, disharmony. To love and work harmoniously, completely, there must be the highest intelligence. This state is without fear, without exploitation and without seeking a reward.

The art of living is to know how to bring this "I" process to an end. It is an art that needs great discernment and right effort. True living is the ending of accumulation. The man who is really living has no sense of accumulation. The man who is seeking security, certainty, shelter, the shelter of character, virtue, that man thinks accumulation is life. To him all of life becomes a process of learning, gaining, struggle. Where there is this idea of accumulation and gain, there must be a sense of time. The past and the future become very important and hence there is incompleteness of action. Incompleteness of action causes conflict.

To live simply is the greatest of arts. It demands deep intelligence and not the superficial comprehension of life. To live intelligently simply one must be free of all those restrictions, resistances, limitations, which each individual has developed for his own self-protection and which have hindered his true relationship with society. These barriers must be understood.

The individual at present is a separate being who is self-conscious, who thinks that he is different from another, in whom there is the separation of "you and me." However, in truth, in him is the totality of all experience, all thought, all emotion. He is the world and the world is him. The individual is the focus of the universe; he is the whole universe, the whole world, not a separate part of the world.

However, to be truly an individual is to be in the state in which there is no separateness, no individuality. It is pure being, which is dynamic, not static, which is neither the annihilation nor the continuity of the individual but which is the ending of the ego of reaction.

When you begin to free yourself from all social influences, the true individual is born. This freedom takes place only when the mind begins to see where the false is and therefore rejects it. Then only is there an individuality, which is not resisting, which is not opposition to society, an individuality not based on resistance or acquisition, but which has understood the false. This energy releases the energy, which acts to free man from the false. In such an individual this energy will operate on society, and the individual's responsibility is entirely different. Then it will act, not in terms of disowning or modifying society, but out of its own understanding, its own vitality, which comes through the discovery of that which is false. Then there can be action, which will be effective in the transformation of society. This comes about by recollectedness, by constant awareness, by dedication with this purpose ever in mind in all that you are doing.

312

CHAPTER 42

Truth

*Truth is unique. It is complete. Truth is a reality that cannot be
understood by following a path, an ideology, a religious doctrine
or any system. Wisdom, truth, is in the understanding of the
real and living in that reality.*

Most people think that truth is hidden away from general existence, from the ordinary human mind, from the ordinary man of thought and feeling. They imagine that they must retire from the world to seek truth, that they must acquire certain qualities, experience sorrows and certain pleasures. The moment you understand life as it is taking place in you and about you, then you will understand the true, truth.

Our usual search for truth is but an escape. Our studies of philosophies, our pursuit of truth through organized religions, our gathering of religious ideas, forms, methods, and our continual groping for reality, are ways of escape.

Truth does not lie in the choice of the essential as against the unessential. Truth does not exist in the opposites. What is chosen cannot be true, for opposites are merely the interplay of reactions. There cannot be your truth and my truth; there is only truth. You can understand its unique quality only when the mind is free of "yours" and "mine." The "you" and the "me" are memories, based on self-protective and accumulative reactions. When you begin to perceive the illusion of choice itself, that revelation is liberating, spontaneously destroying the illusion upon which the "I" nourishes itself. When the mind is free from the sense of "mine" and "yours" then there is life, there is truth.

Truth is experience dissociated from the past. The attachment to the past with its memories, traditions, is the continuance of a static center, the self, which prevents the experience of truth.

Truth cannot be explained or described. It is. You can know it only when you have understood the full significance of that which is before you.

Truth alone can free each one from the sorrow and confusion of ignorance. Truth is not the end of experience, it is life itself. It is not of tomorrow, it is of no time. It is not a result, an achievement, but the cessation of fear and want. Truth is not a finality that can be attained through certain actions. It is that understanding born of continual adjustment to life, which demands great intelligence. Because people are not capable of this self-defenseless adjustment to the movement of life, they create certain theories and ideals, which they hope will guide them to the truth.

Truth is unique. It is complete. Truth is a reality that cannot be understood by following a path, an ideology, a religious doctrine or any system. Wisdom, truth, is in the understanding of the real and living in that reality.

To understand truth is to understand the cause of our conflicts and sufferings.

Truth is awareness, constant awareness of life within us and about us. Truth is nothing abstract. It is neither philosophy, occultism nor mysticism. It is everyday life. It is perceiving the meaning and wisdom of life around us. The only life worth dealing with is our present life and every one of its moments. What matters is that we should live completely at every moment of our lives. That is the only real liberation. But to understand it, you must liberate your mind from all memories and allow it to meet spontaneously the present moment. There can be no other spontaneity of life; and that is precisely what is called awareness, truth.

Awareness established in ourselves dispels ignorance and fear. If you make an effort to be aware, then that effort creates habit and a hope of escape from sorrow. Then you will be using self-knowledge to achieve a result, which will only create greater self-consciousness. But where there is deep and choiceless awareness, there is self-revelation, which alone can prevent the mind from creating illusions for itself and thereby putting itself to sleep. If there is constant alertness of mind without the duality of the observer and the observed, without the thinker and his thought, if mind can know itself as it is, without denial, assertion, acceptance or resignation, then out of that very actuality there comes love, creative intelligence, truth.

A Glimpse into the Life of Hugh and Marjorie Keller

Hugh Walter Keller was an osteopathic physician as well as served in the US Navy. Marjorie Keller became an earnest seeker of truth and a devoted student of Krishnamurti in her early twenties.

The couple met in Los Angeles, and traveled to Ojai, California frequently to listen to the teachings of Krishnamurti, one of the greatest thinkers and teachers of all time. Eventually, they moved to Arya Vihara in Ojai, to dive deeper into the teachings.

Dr. Keller became one of Krishnamurti's physicians. During their time together, they would frequently take walks in deep conversations. Through their intimate friendship and Dr. Keller's understanding of the teachings, he began writing his book, *Transformation*, approximately seventy years ago. Hubert Walter Keller passed away in April 1971.

Marjorie Keller lived most of her life in the Taormina Community of Ojai. She was a devout student of

Mr. and Mrs. Keller

Krishnamurti and a member of the Theosophical Society for most of her life. She spent her life in deep devotion to spiritual awakening, living in the ashrams of India and traveling the world in search of truth. She had three children, who were fortunate to attend the Krishnamurti schools in Ojai, England, and India.

This book, a sacred family treasure, was first printed in India in 1976 by Marjorie Keller. During her final days, her daughter, Jaya Sarada, was asked by her mother to publish it through her publishing company, Divine Light Publishing.

The tree that was planted in the oak grove in memory of my mother Marjorie Keller.
— Jaya Sarada

The moment you have in your heart this extraordinary thing called love and feel the depth, the delight, the ecstasy of it, you will discover that for you the world is transformed.

– Jiddu Krishnamurti

Please visit the Krishnamurti Foundation of America for more information about the teachings of J. Krishnamurti.

https://www.kfa.org/

Cover photo by D. Wadia, Krishnamurti in 1948.

Courtesy of Krishnamurti Foundation of America (KFA) ©KFA

www.ingramcontent.com/pod-product-compliance
Lightning Source LLC
Chambersburg PA
CBHW052354030726
47599CB00014B/1059